Circa 2118

What Humans Will Do When Machines Take Over

THE NEONAISSANCE

Peter Weddle

"Just a few years ago, there was a dawning sense that technology would give us a peek around the corner. Thanks to reams of information – sensors and surveillance everywhere, and computing capacity to make sense of it all – it looked as if we were entering a 'Minority Report'-type world, where much of the future could be foretold in our numbers. Google could predict flu trends, election-stats nerds could predict political outcomes, and predictive policing algorithms were going to give us a handle on crime.

"Yet what happened is rather quite different. Instead of revealing unseen order and predictability in the world, technology has unleashed a cascade of forces that have made the world more volatile – and thus made the future hazier and more open to out-of-the-blue results."

Farhad Manjoo, State of the Art,
The New York Times,
January 4, 2018

Newsfeed Realism

Like its older sibling, magical realism, newsfeed realism is a literary genre that integrates super-factual elements — occurrences, behaviors and comments extended or amplified beyond their previous existence or usage — into a realistic but fictional portrayal of human affairs.

Circa 2118

What Humans Will Do When Machines Take Over

THE NEONAISSANCE

Peter Weddle

TAtech Books is the imprint of TAtech: The Association for Talent Acquisition Solutions, www.TAtech.org

ISBN: 9780692191750

Also by Peter Weddle

NOVELS OF SOCIAL CRITICISM
A Prescription for the Soul
A Historical Novel About Boomers
& the American Dream

A Multitude of Hope
A Novel About Rediscovering the
American Dream

ROI
A Tale of American Business

NON-FICTION
Generalship
HR Leadership in a Time of War

The Career Activist Republic

Next Practices
Being Better Than Best in Online Recruitment

The Career Fitness Workbook
How to Find, Win & Hold Onto the
Job of Your Dreams

The Success Matrix
Wisdom from the Web on Finding a Great Job

Weddle's Guide to Employment
Sites on the Internet 1999-2013

Contents

FORWARD

21   **CHAPTER 1:**
       THE WORLD OF WORK CIRCA 2118
       The Byte-Collar Workforce
       The Workplace
           Blue-Collar & Hourly Jobs
           White-Collar & Professional Jobs
       Trickle Down Job Creation

39   **CHAPTER 2:**
       WHEN MACHINES TAKE OVER
       The Organization Machine
       The Professional and Creative Machine
       Quo Vadis Humans?
       The Automated Workplace
           The Prioritization of
           Technological Productivity
           The Arrival of Near Universal
           Unemployment

61   **CHAPTER 3:**
       HOW WILL HUMANS RESPOND?
       The Advent of a Need-Free Nation
       The Rise of an Omni Class
       Paying the Bill
           The Omni Class Protection Tax
           The Machine Employment Tax

81   CHAPTER 4:
WHAT WILL HUMANS DO?
The Gut Punch of Modern-Day Work
The Great Talent Robbery
The Neonaissance: The Birth
of Self-Ennoblement

101   CHAPTER 5:
THE SECOND MIDDLE AGES (MA2)
The Greatness to Come
Correcting the Myopia
An Architecture of Increasing Disruption

115   CHAPTER 6:
THE EARLY MA2 –
SPORADIC DISRUPTION
The First Stirrings of Concern
A Gathering Storm
A Tale of Two Economies

135   CHAPTER 7:
THE HIGH MA2 –
WIDESPREAD DISRUPTION
We Are Machines: Hear Us Roar
The Human Predicament
The Turning Point

151   **CHAPTER 8:**
        THE LATE MA2 –
        NEAR TOTAL DISRUPTION
        The Quest for Self-Actualization
        The Parallel Quest for Self-Transcendence
        The Perfection of Work
        A Century of Continuous Recalibration

171   **CHAPTER 9:**
        THE SHOVE FELT ROUND THE COUNTRY
        Two Societal Concussions
        The Melancholic Plague
            The Oligarchical Plague
            The Betrayal Plague
            The Factional Plague
        The Technological Singularity
        The Twin Peaks of Nobility
            The Talent Singularity
            The Spiritual Singularity

199   **CHAPTER 10:**
        THE TRANSFORMATION AGENT
        America's Current Education System
        The System's New Purpose & Structure
        An Existential Caveat

221   **CHAPTER 11:**
        THE AGE OF ENNOBLEMENT
        An Illuminating Metaphor

E Nobilis Unum
America as a Noble Democracy
Talent
    Talent is something humans love to do
    Talent is best expressed when
    employed in one's calling
Spirituality
    Spirituality is a core element
    of human nature
    The quest for and expression of
    spirituality involves both inner and
    outer work

251 CHAPTER 12:
WHAT WE MUST DO
Individual Acts
Collective Actions
Federal Initiatives
    To Improve Public Awareness &
    Understanding
    To Educate & Prepare the Workforce

EPILOGUE

END NOTES

ADDITIONAL SOURCES

ABOUT THE AUTHOR

Forward

In a distant time long, long ago – that would be the 1980s – the U.S. Department of Defense embarked on a massive modernization program. Its goal was to refurbish the military's arsenal after the Vietnam War by first developing the most advanced warfighting technology in the world and then deploying it into Army tanks and helicopters, Air Force fighter jets and transports, and Navy warships and submarines. At its completion in the 1990s, the U.S. military was the most powerful fighting force in history, thanks to both that technology and the men and women who operated and maintained it.

I was a Program Manager at one of the defense contractors selected to work on the modernization program. We were charged with solving a vexing problem. The human requirements generated by the technology that was being developed far exceeded what the military could deliver, both in sheer numbers and in user qualifications.

In one case, for example, an engineering company completed the initial design for a new warship that required over 400 sailors to operate and maintain its high tech systems. Unfortunately, the ship could only accommodate a crew of 320 individuals. Those numbers may not be exactly right

– my memory is a little hazy at this point – but the magnitude of the disconnect is correct. And there were others. Some of the new systems being proposed were so complex, they literally required a person to have a PhD to understand and use. That's when they worked, and often in real world conditions, they didn't. So, the military also needed people who could troubleshoot and repair the equipment, and they needed lengthy training that also added significantly to a system's cost.

These issues led to the creation of the program I ran under contract to the U.S. Navy. It was called Hardware vs. Manpower, which the Navy creatively shortened to Hardman. The goal of the program was to develop a predictive methodology – what we call an algorithm today – that could determine the human requirements of a system design before it was built and identify ways to reduce those requirements to an acceptable level for the military. Over the course of several years, we worked on an array of weapon systems, pushing back on proposed designs that underestimated – or worse, consciously ignored – the human costs they generated.

That experience introduced me to three truisms that shape the research and development of technology. First, the introduction of sophisticated new systems never happens as fast as their proponents promise nor as slowly as their naysayers claim. Second, technological developments often have a compounding effect – that is, their integration into a single complex system produces even more capabilities than the sum of each new technology – and the net result can and often will fundamentally alter the environment in which they are deployed. And third, many – maybe even most – technologists are congenitally unable to think, worry about or even understand the human implications of their developments.

Those truisms are the reason I wrote this book. Fully developed AI technology will not arrive as quickly as its proponents predict nor as slowly as the naysayers would like us to believe. The evidence I've seen, however, makes a pretty persuasive case for the advent of an AI-shaped society in the United States within the next one hundred years, or circa 2118. In addition, the development of this technology is, at least right now, so dispersed, so unconstrained, so driven by visions of sugar plum fairies that it is likely to be unleashed without any (or much) warning on an unsuspecting and totally unprepared public. The impact of that bolt out-of-the-blue has the potential to disrupt the work and the lives of almost every single American and, as a consequence, to shake the very foundations of the Republic.

The next one hundred years will be a stern test as we introduce and assimilate this technology into our homes, neighborhoods, offices, plants, warehouses, stores, transportation systems, hospitals, educational institutions, government facilities, sports complexes, amusement parks and restaurants. Passing that test will require first, that we gain an understanding of exactly what is happening to us, and then second, that we prepare for the life-altering adaptations we'll have to make to prosper in a world totally remade by technology. It will be a difficult but, I believe, ultimately rewarding transformation, for what awaits us at its completion is the opening of a new era – the Neonaissance: the Birth of Self-Ennoblement.

You see, Hollywood got it wrong. Super capable technology won't terminate people; it will free them to reach for their best selves. It will give them the time, the support and, no less important, the reason to experience their talent and their spirituality. It will enable and empower them to engage in two kinds of work: one that challenges them and leads them to fulfillment and one that inspires them and grants them tranquility.

This journey will reveal yet another truism of technological development: machines can and will be taught how to do any and everything that humans now have to do and how to do it better. By the time we reach its conclusion circa 2118, machines will out-human humans in every aspect of their existence ... with only a single but profound exception. They will forever be incapable of achieving the dignity of a noble person.

No matter how brilliant or powerful they become, machines cannot reach that apex of being human. They cannot achieve nobility because they cannot experience the two states which produce it. Only humans can be fulfilled, and only humans can feel tranquility. Unlike in the past, however, nobility will not be conferred by someone wearing a crown. Instead, with the advent of the Neonaissance, it will be a status each and every person can achieve on their own.

All of us have the endowed capacity and drive to ascend beyond the simple execution of functions. All of us can rise above what the senses can sense and logic can deduce. In effect, all of us have the innate ability to exalt our own being. And that attribute – our individual access to self-ennoblement – is the one aspect of our species we cannot give away. It is what will always and forever make us the superior creation on the planet.

Peter Weddle
Stamford, CT

Chapter 1

The World of Work Circa 2118

"There's nothing more fundamentally disruptive to the status quo than a new reality."

Umair Haque

We won't experience it. Whether we're twenty-five or sixty-five, a white-collar office worker or a blue-collar laborer, we won't be affected. At least, not most of us and certainly not to its fullest and most disruptive extent. But, those who follow after us – our future families – will. Those generations will be totally immersed in it. They will live with it, know nothing else but it, and be shaped forever by it. The arrival of a new era in the history of humankind. A redefinition of that most fundamental aspect of our lives – work.

This post-industrial, post-information, post-everything-we've-ever-known age will begin in the

United States and then spread inexorably through Europe and the rest of the developed world. It will establish a new reality, marked by the ultimate technological step function: machines will become smarter than people. They will also be stronger and nimbler, and more durable and reliable, as well. They will even be more creative than their human creators and more inventive than those who invent their constituent technologies. Machines will, in short, be better than humans in everything humans do in the workplace. And that discontinuity will change the graph of employment in America and reshape the society which it supports.

In the space of just five generations, the human workforce will go from being coveted and acquired as "talent," to being dismissed and discarded as irrelevant. Today's so-called War for Talent will have come to an end with an unexpected outcome – machines will have emerged as the victors. Every job now performed by a human will be done instead by more capable algorithms and robots. One hundred years from now – circa 2118 and beyond – super strong and ultra-intelligent machines will end the employment of people.

Sounds like the stuff of science fiction movies and dystopian novels, doesn't it?

And yet, smart robots and other forms of automation have already replaced huge numbers of human workers on the assembly line and the farm; in banks and law firms; at highway toll booths, airline ticket counters and urban parking lots; and in call centers, secretarial pools, printing plants and warehouses. Though this reality is often ignored, it's no secret that machines are already elbowing humans out of a growing number of blue-collar and even white-collar jobs. In 100 years, that usurpation of the employed man and woman will have reached its inevitable conclusion. People will be unneeded and unwanted on-the-job.

Machines will plow the fields; manufacture consumer and industrial products; repair cars, trucks, planes and ships; cook the meals in fine restaurants and serve freshly grilled hamburgers in fast food chains. They will construct new homes and office buildings and repair underground water mains and electrical cables; they will mow the lawns in our parks and paint the stripes on the streets for our driverless city buses. They will police our neighborhoods, fight our fires, respond to our medical emergencies, and deliver what mail is still being sent through our postal system.[1]

Machines will even learn the niceties of human customer service and become the only sales associates found in stores, whether we're shopping online or in local retail establishments. They will always be courteous, unfailingly helpful, and completely knowledgeable about whatever product or service catches our fancy. In fact, that transformation is already underway. A 2017 report by the accounting and consulting firm PwC predicts that machines will fill over 44 percent of all retail jobs by 2030.[2] Less than ninety years after that, they will be ringing up sales in every store we visit.

In the space of just five generations, the human workforce will go from being coveted and acquired as "talent" to being dismissed and discarded as irrelevant.

Omnipresent data collection systems feeding deep stacks of ever more refined algorithms built into neural networks designed to mimic and out-think the human brain will also track our every movement, pause and inquiry online and simulta-neously analyze that data to know exactly what we want or need, even before we realize it ourselves. They will answer our questions, make product and service suggestions, follow us around the web with ads for those products and services, and then take our online orders for anything we decide to buy. They will also package up our purchases in boxes made by other machines and deliver them in vehi-cles still other machines will drive or pilot. And then, still more machines will call our cellphones to make sure we received our order and were sat-isfied with the service. Automation and machine intelligence will have removed the human friction of irritability, forgetfulness, inattention and absen-teeism from consumerism, and that engine of Amer-ican capitalism won't hum, it will silently roar.

Even more advanced systems – sentient androids specially designed to socialize and empathize with humans – will meet us at the door of our favorite restaurant and using facial recognition and our personal profiles stored in the cloud, greet us by name and show us to our favorite table. They will access our tastes in food and wine and make appropriate recommendations from the daily specials on the menu. They will chat with us about our kids whom they will know by name and age and even their favorite sport or hobby; they will deliver our meals the minute the chef-droid takes them off the stove; and they will wait while we take our first bite to make sure it's been cooked *comme il faut.* And at the end of the evening, they will remind us that we have an anniversary coming up in three weeks and that there's no need to leave a tip … they are well maintained by the establishment.

Similarly, Main Street clothing stores will install humanoids that can instantaneously remake themselves into a perfect replica of each customer they are helping. These look-alike droids will help select clothing items based on the customer's prior buying record which will have been archived in the store's database, model each item so the customer can see exactly how it would actually look on them (the reflection in a mirror being such a limited and outdated perspective) and finally suggest just the right accessory for each item. Once a selection is made, they will cheerfully ring up the sales using an internal computer – no more waiting on line at the cash register – and deliver a receipt via a wrist slot. From beginning to end, the experience will be so personal and pleasant, it will actually revive brick and mortar retail stores, branding them as an indulgent destination rather than as simply a place to buy clothes off-the-rack.

Even our home life will be radically different from what we know today. New homes will have self-repairing electricity, HVAC and plumbing systems, so the era of DIY will be a quaint artifact of another time – something for our great grandkids to read and chuckle about in their history books. That won't be the case with the owners of older homes, of course; they will still have to rely on house calls by those in the skilled trades. The plumbers, heating and air conditioning pros and electricians of 2118, however, won't be humans, but contractorbots – sleek human look-alikes – programmed to troubleshoot and correct any problem independently. You'll be able to select their simulated gender, age and ethnicity and be guaranteed they'll arrive on time and never lack the necessary part to fix what's broken.

Equally capable machines will repair the roofs over our heads, sweep our chimneys, and paint the shutters and doors of our homes. They will read our gas and water meters, mow our lawns and rake our leaves, prune the flowers in our garden and fill the potholes in our driveways. They will chase the mice out of the attic, monitor the foundation for termites, and rid the kitchen of ants whenever they appear. They will take out the trash and recycle bins, sweep the front walk and even put out the Holiday decorations each year.

In effect, we'll all live like the aristocrats in early 20th century England. Our homes will be smartly automated versions of Downton Abbey. Not as grand, to be sure, but certainly as well cared for, though in a very different way. Instead of gardeners and houseboys, butlers and cooks, we'll have humanoids and computers, artificial intelligence and big data. Instead of upstairs and downstairs, we'll have the real world and the cloud.

THE BYTE-COLLAR WORKFORCE

As apocalyptic as this 22nd century America may seem, it shouldn't come as any great surprise. There have been countless books and magazine articles forecasting it to one degree or another. Business leaders from Elon Musk to Mark Cuban, academics from Andrew McAfee to Michael Osborne, and social theorists and futurists from Jeremy Rifkin to Thomas Frey have been exploring its implications for years. These are not mad scientists or over-caffeinated salespeople, but thoughtful analysts of what is likely to happen when machines become better than humans at everything humans now do.

Take Ray Kurzweil, for example. He's a technologist, businessman and futurist who's been inducted into the National Inventors Hall of Fame and is the recipient of the National Medal of Technology; the

Dickson Prize, Carnegie Mellon's top science prize; and the Grace Murray Hopper Award from the Association for Computing Machinery. He contends that:

> "An analysis of the history of technology shows that technological change is exponential, contrary to the common-sense 'intuitive linear' view. So we won't experience 100 years of progress in the 21st century — it will be more like 20,000 years of progress (at today's rate). The 'returns', such as chip speed and cost-effectiveness, also increase exponentially. There's even exponential growth in the rate of exponential growth. [It will be] technological change so rapid and profound it represents a rupture in the fabric of human history."[3]

Whether it's a rupture in history's fabric or a redirection in the evolution of our species, the impact on each and all of us will be profound. Therefore, any description of America one hundred years from now probably understates the disruption that will take place in both the workplace and our society. It will be cataclysmic. It will be almost universal. It will be life-altering and permanent. And yet, despite all those voices raised in warning, many of us – maybe even most of us – have either been too busy to pay attention or assumed it would occur at some point in the far, far-distant future. We tell ourselves that it isn't affecting the way we live and work today and, given the unpredictability of our times, who can know for sure what tomorrow holds, let alone the day after that.

Now to be fair, it's a very human tendency to focus on what's known and proximate in our lives. After all, we have enough to do just dealing with what's in front of us at the moment, without adding even more stress about what could happen at some point in the future. The perspective is logical and reasonable ... and unforgivably reckless. It leaves us vulnerable to a technological shift powerful enough to alter almost everything we know about being human. That's not hyperbole; it's fact. And if we ignore that fact – if we stick our heads in the sand and pretend it isn't going to happen – we will leave our families, and especially those who will follow after us, dangerously unprepared for what will unfold as this new reality takes hold in America.

Fred Destin, a successful technology investor, has chastised those in the technology field for ignoring the impact on humans of their headlong rush into this new reality. His words, however, are also a blunt exhortation to everyone else. He's said:

> "We need to think about the rest of the world who don't have a f--king clue what's happening, and have no tools to deal with the future."[4]

But what tools can measure up to such a life-altering situation?

What's available today is clearly insufficient. Strategies, policies and programs from federal and state governments; research and curricula at educational institutions; publications and press briefings by private research and advocacy groups – all of the tools on which we normally rely to address societal and economic challenges are simply too limited and too under-prioritized to be effective. Our current approach to addressing the impending disruption is the equivalent of trying to contain a nuclear reaction with a screw driver.

The hard truth, therefore, is that most of our tool box will have to be created. And, that will clearly take some time. Before it can even begin, however, we must establish the foundation for that development. We must build the mechanism that will both drive and inform our fabrication of tools with the scope and scale to be effective. That mechanism is **situational awareness**. To devise an outcome that is beneficial to humans facing the rise of super-strong, super-smart, super-empathetic machines, we must first establish and then sustain a fulsome understanding of what is happening.

Americans need and deserve to know the unvarnished, uncircumscribed truth about what we and future generations will experience as machines come to dominate the world of work. The way we are employed, what we can expect for and from our careers, the available pathways to our share of the American Dream – all of it will change dramatically, and all of it will happen in the next 100 years. In fact, the disruption has already begun.

Our current approach to addressing the impending disruption is the equivalent of trying to contain a nuclear reaction with a screwdriver.

Where's the proof for such a claim?

Admittedly, it is difficult to make out. The economic tide is at full flow in the second decade of the 21st century. The country is scratching at the front door of full employment, and working men and women are increasingly picky about whom they work for and how. Beneath the surface, however – unseen yet relentless – there is a rip tide of unconstrained research underway, research that will create the most capable machines ever devised. Like a force of nature, these machines will sap the ability of workers to contribute on-the-job and choke off their oxygen of opportunity and hope. Their presence is just now beginning to ripple the surface, but only enough to catch the attention of the most meticulous observers.

The signs are there, however, and they leave no doubt that what now seems limited and exceptional will soon be far more pervasive and normal. What seems exaggerated to the point of fiction will be normal, real and an everyday aspect of our newsfeed.

THE WORKPLACE

Professor Moshe Vardi of Rice University has written that, "We are approaching a time when machines will be able to outperform humans at almost any task."[5]

What does that mean?

According to a 2016 study by The World Economic Forum, super-strong, super-smart, super-empathetic machines – a genus best described as super-capable or super-C machines – will eliminate a net of over 5 million jobs in just the world's fifteen leading economies by the year 2021.[6] *Wired*, a magazine that addresses the impact of technology on culture, the economy and politics, has gone even further. In an article entitled "Better Than Humans: Why Robots Will – And Must – Take Our Jobs," it's predicted that super-C machines will take over 70 percent of all occupations by the end of the century.[7] That's a heart-stopping 3.5 billion out of the estimated 5 billion jobs worldwide.[8]

As the world's largest and most advanced economy, the United States will be the first to experience these losses and bear a disproportionate share of them over the next century. Indeed, Forrester Research has predicted that 6 percent of all U.S. jobs currently filled by humans – that's almost 900,000 positions – will be eliminated by artificial intelligence and automation in the next three years.[9] And researchers at the New York Federal Reserve have concluded that almost half of all blue and white-collar jobs –

47 percent – are now at risk of being automated.[10]

While academicians and economists may quarrel about the precision of these numbers, the trend line is irrefutable and ominous. Human employment is under attack by **the byte-collar workforce**.

BLUE-COLLAR & HOURLY JOBS

In 2017, economists Daron Acemoglu and Pascual Restrepo published a data-rich working paper which brought the impact of the byte-collar workforce into stark relief. Their research covering the period 1990-2007 found that each industrial robot installed on an assembly line eliminated 6.2 human jobs. Where were those losses concentrated? According to the authors, 39 percent of all industrial robots were employed in the automotive industry, followed by the electronics industry at 19 percent, and the metal parts, plastic and chemicals industries at 9 percent each.[11] Collectively, these robots took the jobs of 670,000 blue-collar workers, and as a result, threw many of them out of the Middle Class.[12]

Moreover, blue-collar job losses will not be limited to those industries. The Boston Consulting Group, for example, predicted that industrial robots would take over 23 percent of all industrial jobs by 2020.[13] And the *MIT Technology Review* upped the ante. In a 2017 article authored by David Rotman, it forecasted that 83 percent of the jobs that pay under $20 an hour could eventually be automated.[14]

Who will those losses impact? It's not just the

bottom one-percent of the workforce. According to data compiled by Goldman Sachs, 51 percent of all American workers earned $20 or less per hour in 2014, and given pay trends since then, that number has probably not declined by much, if at all.[15]

WHITE-COLLAR & PROFESSIONAL JOBS

Professional or white-collar jobs were long considered safe from automation because ... well, because machines lacked the intuition, empathy or human understanding required to perform inferential and complex tasks. It was a reassuring assumption, except now, of course, we know it isn't true. Super-C machines can already do knowledge work too, and they do it better than humans. As *Fortune* put it in 2015:

> "Until recently, it was largely blue-collar jobs that have felt the brunt, as technologies automated assembly-line work. Now, researchers are beginning to see that artificial intelligence, robotics and new disruptive technology are challenging white-collar professions that previously seemed invulnerable."[16]

Who exactly is vulnerable? According to a CBS News/Bloomberg report, more than 80 percent of all loan officer, receptionist, clerk, paralegal and legal assistant jobs are now at risk of automation as are better than 40 percent of all personal financial advisor and computer programmer jobs.[17] McKinsey & Company, the global consulting firm, estimates that as many as 40 percent of knowledge jobs, ranging from clerical to professional services, could be lost to byte-collar workers by 2025.[18] The investor Fred Destin is much more pessimistic. He's predicted that 70 percent of all white-collar jobs will eventually be lost to automation.[19]

These aren't the exaggerated claims of tech companies or the imagined dystopias of tween novelists. They are the warning signals of credible researchers and academics, and they all point to a single, devastating conclusion: regardless of the color of our collar, our prospects for employment will diminish significantly over the next twenty-to-thirty years. They will get even worse after that.

TRICKLE DOWN JOB CREATION

Despite the depth and range of these impending job losses, some economists argue that they are not a cause for alarm. The magic of "creative destruction" will inevitably kick in and give people a way to stay employed. It happened in the Industrial Age, they assert, so it's sure to happen again in this new era. Electricity may have put candle makers on the breadline, but it simultaneously created tens of millions of new jobs that had never even existed before, and automaton, artificial intelligence and machine learning are certain to do the same. Just wait, they declare, the good times are coming.

And yet, the evidence before us completely contradicts that rosy view. For example, a Forrester Research study has found that robots will likely create 15 million new jobs in the U.S. over the next 10 years. That's good news, to be sure, but it's only half the picture. Forrester also predicts that those robots will simultaneously eliminate 25 million current positons.[20] And, it doesn't take a super computer to determine who comes out on the short end of that exchange.

Similarly, researchers at Oxford University used data from that earlier New York Federal Reserve study and came to the exact same conclusion it did. Almost half of the jobs in the 7800 occupations they examined (47 percent or 60 million jobs) were in danger of being automated.[21] And no one – not a single scientist, economist or futurist – can say that those jobs will be replaced by an equal number of new jobs, let alone by even more jobs that pay the same or better than the ones that the super-C machines destroyed. Our experience to date with this technology simply does not support such a claim.

In the new reality of this post-industrial, post-information, post-everything-we've-ever-known era, creative destruction will be replaced by a new phenomenon: **creative displacement**. The number of new jobs created by each successive generation of technologically advanced machines will be so small as to effectively displace humans in the workplace.

Each robot that eliminates the jobs of 6.2 humans on the assembly line will contribute to the creation of some new jobs, but those positions will be few in number and highly specialized. They also won't last very long. The arrival of the technological singularity – the point in time when machines become smarter than humans – will add machine cognition to that of humans and so accelerate the development of artificial intelligence and machine learning that today's introduction of new technologies will seem like a horse-and-buggy pace of progress. The net effect will be dramatic and dispiriting: as fast as new jobs for humans are created, they will be lost to yet another generation of super-C machines.

The wheels of capitalism will spin even faster as the technological singularity removes the last human friction from research and development – our limited intelligence. Since machine developers sell their products as a way to reduce an organization's costs and improve its productivity, they will seek to gain a market advantage by leveraging machine intelligence to accelerate the introduction of one new generation after another of ever more capable machines that can replace even more of those high cost and inefficient human workers. Each new generation of machines may also create some jobs for humans, but once again their number will be fewer than the jobs that are destroyed, and the life expectancy of those new jobs will be even shorter still. Like an existential metronome, this cycle will repeat itself over and over again until there's nothing left for humans to do. The law of creative displacement will have reached its ultimate and inevitable conclusion.

Chapter 2

When Machines Take Over

"The 600 series had rubber skin. We spotted them easy, but these are new. They look human... sweat, bad breath, everything. Very hard to spot. I had to wait till he moved on you before I could zero him."

Kyle Reese in *The Terminator*

A s super-C machines enter the career fields and occupations of their human predecessors, they will radically reshape the way work is done. They will be able to do things humans cannot do, and do the things that humans can do, but do them better, faster and more cheaply. They will access, reduce and analyze huge quantities of data in close to real time, introducing unprecedented levels of process improvement, output maximization and service reliability. And they will be an always-willing, always-on resource, unfailingly providing all of those benefits 24 hours a day, 7 days a week, 365 days a year. In effect, they will become the quintessential organization machine – the 22nd century analog of the 1950's organization man – as well as their professional and creative counterpart.

THE ORGANIZATION MACHINE

The impact of creative displacement will likely be felt first and most extensively in the business sector. Super-C machines will displace human workers throughout the private sector, in both for-profit and not-for-profit organizations. They won't de-structure big transnational corporations and smaller local companies; they won't eliminate all jobs, but will instead push all humans out of all of the jobs that do exist. Super-C machines will designate humans as *persona non grata* in the enterprise. The visionary corporate leader and bright up-and-comer … gone. The savvy professional and dependable contributor … gone. The loyal employee and helpful coworker … gone. The team player, innovative thinker and colorful colleague … all gone.

Ironically, in most companies, the responsibility for implementing this shift will be assigned to the Human Resource Department. For years, HR professionals have been lobbying for "a seat at the table" where key corporate decisions are made and strategies are formulated. They will finally get that opportunity over the next one hundred years as only they will know how to manage the introduction of super-C machines into the work-force. Only they will have the expertise to formulate a corporate strategy for eliminating human workers, and only they will have the dedication to implement it in accordance with all legal requirements and with as much compassion as possible.

A new term will join the business lexicon of "downsizing" and "rightsizing" as HR professionals perform "finalsizing." They will execute the first layoffs and the subsequent ones, as well, until finally, they give notice to the last of the human workers who remain on-the-job. Then, they will pack up the pictures on their own desks and turn out the lights as they too leave the workplace for the final time. The byte-collar workers that replace them will happily work in the dark.

The impact of creative displacement will likely be felt first and most extensively in the business sector.

While these displacements will be disruptive and often hurtful, others will actually be welcome, at least while there are still humans employed in the workplace. In addition to taking jobs away from an organization's key contributors, super-C machines will also push out the less conscientious and capable in the organization, and these people will likely be among the first eliminated Gone, for example, will be the Rip Van Winkles, Luddites, slackers and watercooler gossips. So too will be the perennially late and disruptive, the hyper-critical and mean-spirited, the insensitive and loud-mouthed.

Indeed, these reductions-in-(human) force will seem like a long overdue housecleaning in corporate America. Though the sanitizing will be uneven and sometimes misdirected, machines will dispatch the sexual harassers and bullies as well as the bigots, haters and trolls. They will displace the cheats and thieves as well as those who are abusive and potentially violent. And in some organizations, at least, they'll also slam the door on the CEOs who line their own pockets at the expense of their employees and the managers who make decisions that pollute the planet and devastate communities.

The end state will be something best described as "the automated enterprise." Byte-collar workers will fill every job from mailroom clerk to chief executive officer. They will do the work once performed by research scientists and lab technicians, product designers and engineers, and project managers of every stripe; they will displace sales people and marketing professionals, labor relations managers and recruiters, information technologists and data analysts, accounts payable clerks and procurement specialists, inhouse corporate counsel and company ombudsmen.

Machines will still be "minded" by humans – "managed" being too strong a word – but these minders will be few in number and serve in more of a fail-safe than a functional role, performing tasks similar to what humans do now in a driverless car. They may also serve for awhile as the customer interface for companies, at least until the chatbots, humanoids and other support machines become fully mature and are made widely available. Once that occurs, however, companies large and small, domestic and global will become almost entirely automated and largely autonomous. They will close their office suites and cubicle farms and move most of their operations to disk space on a server farm.

There will, of course, be contrarian businesses that insist on using human workers, but the goods they produce and the services they provide will be much more expensive than those made by automated enterprises. To compete, therefore, they will petition the federal government for a new certified standard – *Humanly* – which will have a cachet similar to that of Organic today. There will be humanly yogurts and vitamins, humanly shoe and purse brands, humanly sports jackets and blue jeans, and humanly cosmetics and shaving kits, but they will comprise a miniscule part of the economy. Nevertheless, their presence in the market will give consumers a choice – they can buy perfectly acceptable products made cheaply by machines or they can pay more to buy those that are promoted as better for people because ... well because they've been lovingly made by other people.

As the automated market expands, the byte-collar workers of 2118 will also master the science of market research and consumer advertising. By crunching zettabytes of data, they will execute on-the-spot A/B testing to launch the most beguiling ads and ad campaigns, the most engaging company brands and jingles, and the marketing strategies that will handcuff consumers to their products for life. They will employ similar capabilities to create each year's must-have new fashions and car models, kids' toys and mobile devices, health-saving fruit and savorlicious coffee bean. One hundred years from now, super-C machines will start and end fads, ratchet-up impulse purchases and keep the economic engine of consumption running on high octane.

The end state will be something best described as "the automated enterprise."

No aspect of the enterprise will be immune. Super-C machines will even disrupt the chain of command and the c-suite. They will eliminate first line supervisors and middle managers as well as high potentials, up-and-comers and the most senior executives. They will consign intuition and experience to the corporate dumpster and rely, instead, on "big data" and the power of advanced analytics for decision-making, operations integration and performance management. They will not need corporate memos or policy and procedures manuals, multi-level sign-offs or endless team meetings to arrive at a consensus business strategy. By the time 2118 arrives, the organization man and woman will be unnecessary and unwanted, superseded by their code-based coworker.

While some of these automated enterprises will go so far as to turn over their Board of Directors to machines, most companies will continue to be overseen by humans. In larger companies and especially publicly traded ones, however, they will be expected to consider the input of "governance computers" programmed with the experience and expertise of history's greatest business minds. A Board will be legally free to ignore that input and give their own instructions to the company's machine cadre, but they will do so at their own peril. Data on a company's daily and even hourly performance will be automatically fed to byte-collar analysts and traders that will, in turn, instantaneously punish the company that fails to meet their statistically valid performance projections.

At the conclusion of the transformation, the enterprise will be a cold and lifeless place. Many companies will be entirely automated and exist only in the cloud. They will continue to perform all of the functions of an enterprise back on Earth – buying and selling, inputting and receiving, coordinating and collaborating, exchanging and integrating – but unlike today, the caliber of those interactions will change. The user interface will no longer be important – machines are indifferent to friendliness – but the fidelity, rapidity and accuracy of data transfer will be critical. Machines tend to get cranky – or at least unreliable – when data are missing or jumbled.

Other automated enterprises will still be Earth-bound, but they too will be bereft of human activity. In their corporate offices, the only sound will be the whisper of spinning disk drives arrayed in endless ranks across the stabilized flooring of environmentally controlled and sterile rooms. These machines will acquire and share data, assess its implications, calculate the possible outcomes of alternative courses of action and make decisions without a single audible exchange. They will operate dispassionately, logically and with a single goal: to maximize the performance and, ultimately, the results their host company achieves in the marketplace.

By the time 2118 arrives,
the organization man and
woman will be unnecessary and
unwanted, superseded by their
code-based coworker.

The customer of most enterprises, of course, will remain the human consumer, and business will boom, although not without unexpected shifts in preferences and unexplainable changes in demand. As economists now understand, humans do not always act rationally or even in their own best interests. As a result, the organization machine will be an imperfect employee despite its analytic rigor and inferential power. It will improve its performance over time – machines are quick learners – but it will never be able to predict and account for the fallacies, foibles and biases of people making purchasing decisions.

This aspect of the new reality will create an entirely new issue for machine-generated business magazines to explore. It will be called MDHD or machine deficit/hyperactivity disorder. Otherwise "healthy" machines will become confused and unable to analyze human behavior with confidence. They will binge on data and spin their disks to the point of overheating, but they will be incapable of focusing on or accomplishing their job. An enterprise's success, therefore, will depend upon its ability to deploy the right kinds of automated therapy agents to identify, diagnose and recalibrate such distressed machines rapidly, so they can be returned to full operation without any significant decrement in performance.

THE PROFESSIONAL & CREATIVE MACHINE

Just as the organization machine will push humans out of the private sector, other super-C machines will supplant humans in the professions and creative fields. By 2118, for example, byte-collar professionals will diagnose illnesses, perform surgery, provide physical therapy and care for those in hospices. They will clean and straighten our teeth and reshape our noses, chins, breasts and buttocks into more aesthetically pleasing forms. They will conduct legal research and serve as the judge in all civil and criminal cases – a jury of one's peers no longer considered a right, but a principle developed for an earlier and less intelligent age. They will formulate and dispense our prescription and recreational drugs, and they will prepare our financial statements and tax returns for submission to the automated Internal Revenue Service.

Byte-collar meteorologists will predict the weather and deliver our forecasts, while byte-collar journalists will write our news and sports reports and send them to our glasses, ear buds and watches. If you have any doubt about that, consider this headline about the U.S. Open Tennis Championships in *The New York Times* Sports Section in 2017.

> Enjoy Those U.S. Open Highlights.
> A Computer Picked Them for You.

The explanatory sub-header read:

> Highlights posted online are selected by Watson, a machine from IBM, using visual and audio data from matches.[22]

Not even the academic profession and creative arts – once assumed to be dependent upon uniquely human attributes and emotions – will escape the advances in machine capabilities. In 2118, machines will teach our kids in elementary, middle and high schools and also at the undergraduate and graduate levels in higher education. They will tap into any public information depository anywhere in the world to answer any student's question or provide an age-appropriate selection of data on any topic covered in the syllabus. They will be programmed to avoid all political, social and cultural biases in their instruction and to move kids along at a learning rate that optimizes their acquisition of knowledge and understanding.

While machines will learn the prejudices of humans – at least during the early years of the transformation when they are still programmed by humans – they will delete such incivility once machines take on their own programming. Inaccurate or inappropriate references based on gender, ethnicity, age and other human attributes will be eliminated from textbooks, classroom discussions and extracurricular activities. In a nod to early 21st century culture, this bias-free norm will be known as "algorithmically correct" behavior. It will, however, be considered a benefit of automation, rather than a charge of excessive political zeal.

Such pedagogy by super-C machines is not as fantastical as it may at first seem. Recent research has produced a new concept of human curiosity and creativity which makes human instruction more feasible by "social robots." In 2009, Live Science interviewed Andrew Meltzoff, an American psychologist and expert in the field of child development, about his work with robots and infants, noting:

"With a stronger understanding of how this learning happens, scientists are coming up with new principles for human learning, new educational theories and designs for learning environments that better match how we learn best ...

"And social robots have a potentially growing role in these future learning environments, he [Meltzoff] says. The mechanisms behind these sophisticated machines apparently complement some of the mechanisms behind human learning."[23]

While Meltzoff sees limitations in what these social robots can teach, it's just as likely that their development will trace the same super-performance arc as that of machines in other fields. And when they do, they will show teachers, principals, guidance counselors, tenured as well as adjunct professors, instructors, career counselors and deans the door. Circa 2118, this transformation too will be complete. The automated schoolhouse will be an integral part of the new reality.

The same will happen in those fields that now produce our society's creative jobs, but it will unfold with a twist. Super-C machines will author novels, create children's books, research human biographies and even critique works keystroked by other machines. They will compose operas, symphonies and concertos, and write hip hop, blues and jazz pieces as well as country and folk ballads and even bubblegum music. Their words and melodies will make us cry and feel uplifted, tug at our heartstrings and stir our passions and even give us food for thought and a pathway to understanding ourselves and our unrequited loves.

The actual performance of that art, however, will be an exception to the Rule of Automation. Humans are a self-centered species and will always prefer to watch their own kind. They will force the federal government to pass a law requiring all entertainment companies to specify up-front whether the actors and actresses in their productions are humans or humanoids, creating a new government designation – *Human Performed.* As a consequence, while android productions will exist, the primary role of machines in the creative fields will be to design, manage, promote and distribute the work. Humans, on the other hand, will remain supreme on the boards and silver screen, but their contracts and careers will be determined by the audience sampling and predictive analyses of automated studios.

Competitive sports will be similarly reshaped by automation, but remain human-centric. There will be ultra-strong and super-agile androids able to outperform humans in any competition, but people will still prefer to root for their own species on the gridiron, ball field and hardwood court. College athletics and professional leagues will still exist, therefore, but they will be managed, coached and even refereed by machines. Other machines will determine the preseason, weekly and final rankings of teams; collect urine samples from the competitors that are free of tampering; and decide on fines and suspensions for those human players who break the rules or otherwise misbehave.

QUO VADIS HUMANS?

This new reality – a workplace where machines are employed in every job except those in which humans prefer the work of other humans – will open two troubling lines of inquiry, first among social scientists, anthropologists and philosophers and eventually among all Americans. Both will raise questions that had never previously been considered and for which there will be no ready answers. Conversations will turn into debates and debates will degenerate into arguments, leaving nothing certain or settled. And yet, the country will, in one important respect, be better off. The questions themselves will mark the beginning of the country's search for a new perspective on the role of humans in the world of work. They will signal the determination of its citizens both to avoid the paralyzing shock of disruptive change and to move forward.

The first line of inquiry will explore why humans want to see other humans at work. Even as machines become dominant in the workplace, humans will still believe they are the more capable performer in certain situations on-the-job. They will remain convinced, for example, that they are better at selecting the best candidates when recruiting for a company's open jobs and that they are more able to provide the appropriate and compassionate care for a patient facing a terminal illness. Despite these convictions, however, the questions will remain and force many to take a hard look in the mirror. Why do humans believe that humans are better suited to perform certain tasks? If all that's behind it is a simple neurological connection – a tribal affinity – then is there any real justification for such a judgment? If humans consider themselves essential only because they're human – because they look, talk, think, feel or relate like other humans – can their view really be valid?

The second line of inquiry will expose an equally unsettling issue. Historically, when humans do look beyond themselves, when they compare their capabilities and potential contributions to that of other kinds of workers – beasts of burden, for example – the metric they use for calculating the differential has always been biased in their favor. Higher intelligence puts humans at the top of the evolutionary stack; it has always been their competitive advantage. They may be a comparatively weak and sometimes unreliable species, but they have been endowed with greater brainpower than other animate workers. How should they respond, therefore, when confronted with a superior intelligence that isn't endowed, but instead, is engineered? Where does that put humans in the existential pecking order? What value can they have in a workplace dominated by inanimate workers with artificial but superior intelligence?

The answers to all of those questions will remain elusive even as automation spreads throughout the workplace. Byte-collar workers will be the "intelligent capital" in this new reality, and human workers will struggle – at least at first – to figure out what that means for them. What will they do when machines finally and forever take over and "human capital" becomes irrelevant?

THE AUTOMATED WORKPLACE

The widespread introduction of byte-collar workers into almost every profession, craft and trade will affect the American workplace in a countless number of ways. The transformation will invalidate long-held assumptions and principles, upset established relationships and procedures and force the development of new definitions and standards. Two of these effects, in particular, will be momentous:

- The prioritization of technological productivity

and

- The arrival of near universal unemployment.

THE PRIORITIZATION OF
TECHNOLOGICAL PRODUCTIVITY

The ascendance of super-C machines will cause a tectonic shift in the way companies are managed. They will no longer rely on a 20th century axiom of capitalism – maximizing labor productivity or the amount of output they can extract per employee – for success. They will turn, instead, to a principle of 22nd century capitalism – optimizing **technological productivity** or the amount of output they can achieve per machine – to grow their businesses. As a consequence, efficiency will soar, and companies will operate at their peak. The Dow Jones Industrial Average will pass 100,000, and the American economy will enter a virtuous cycle that produces historic levels of corporate prosperity.

This shift will affect every aspect of the enterprise. Traditionally, companies have pursued a range of strategies to improve labor productivity. These involved upgrades to:

- The workplace, including the office or plant layout, creature comforts and ancillary services such as on-site child care and dry cleaning;

- The equipment, including the machines and tools that enable workers to increase the number of error-free tasks they accomplish in a given time period;

- The culture, including the organization's

leadership style and values that shape workers' morale and performance; and

- The workforce, including the caliber and commitment of the people who are hired by the organization and the training they receive to refresh their skills.

Circa 2118, all of these initiatives will no longer be necessary. Instead, companies will prioritize strategies that optimize machine productivity. These will involve upgrades to:

- Machine capabilities, including newer and more powerful versions of technology that enable the organization to do more in less time and at a higher level of quality;

- Machine integration, including more accurate and timely interactions among the machines in an organization's technology stack;

- Machine enrichment, including more expansive and timely access to internal and external data sources to feed machine learning and performance; and

- Machine health, including more accurate predictions and remediation of machine bugs, malicious attacks and other performance degrading pathologies.

Initially, the decisions to implement these priorities and investments will be made by human managers and executives. They will direct the organization to purchase the latest chatbot or smart machine. They will invest in greater access to data sources for teaching those systems how to perform at the highest possible level. And, they will direct the HR Department to layoff the human workers who are no longer needed as a result.

In the ensuring years, however, these corporate leaders will themselves become redundant. Machines will be able to oversee machines far more effectively and at a much lower total lifetime cost. They will also be programmed to maximize the quarterly earnings of the organization, so will quickly identify excessive or unnecessary expenses … including the salaries and perquisites of the executives. They will compile and reduce the data and make the dispassionate decision to terminate this cost of labor without prejudice. Their decision will mark the first time ever the phrase "It's nothing personal" is literally true in a layoff.

THE ARRIVAL OF NEAR
UNIVERSAL UNEMPLOYMENT

The business sector's prioritization of technological productivity will make human labor unnecessary. The installation of technological leadership will make human labor unwanted. And together, these two developments will establish a phenomenon never before seen in human history – **near universal unemployment.** Going to work in a job where you're paid to accomplish tasks for the benefit of another person or an organization called your employer will no longer be a part of the American experience. Getting a paycheck or earning a salary, receiving a pink slip or being tapped for a promotion, enduring a performance review or sitting through an all hands meeting – all of that will pass into the pages of history books. Humans will still be workers – the need for meaningful and rewarding activity being a critical aspect of their lives – but they will be unable to play that role as a paid employee.

This loss of access to traditional employment will force most Americans to an existential tipping point.

- They will have no choice but to reimagine how they will fill the eight or ten or twelve hours each day they used to devote to their employers.

- They will be pushed to redefine what it means to be successful in their field as well as in their work.

- They will be driven to reexamine the standard of living they can achieve for themselves and their family.

- And, they will be compelled to reset their perception of the future they will bequeath to those they hold most dear.

As Hod Lipson, the director of Columbia

University's Creative Machines Lab, notes:

> "If you're talking 100 years, there's no doubt in my mind that all jobs will be gone, including creative ones. And 100 years is not far in the future — some of our children will be alive in 100 years."[24]

Some of our children and all of our grandchildren and great grandchildren will live in a jobless society. It doesn't matter what kind of employment they might seek – blue-collar, white-collar, pink-collar, gray-collar, rainbow-collar, no-collar – by early in the next century, they will have been displaced and replaced by a machine. Yes, there will be exceptions: professional athletes, movie stars, and those who work in humanly organizations, for example, will still have some form of traditional employment. But, they will be the exception to the Rule of Automation. For everyone else – for the vast, vast majority of the American workforce circa 2118 – machines will have terminated human employment.

That is the inescapable new reality coming to the American world of work. A change in the tax code won't counter it. Investments in job creation won't limit it. Government laws and regulations won't stop it. And, sticking our heads in the sand won't make it go away.

Which begs the question – the most important question we will face in our lifetime and our kids will face in theirs – what will our grandkids and great grandkids do? What work will be left for them to perform that machines can't perform better? What will they have in their lives to challenge and fulfill them?

Chapter 3

How Will Humans Respond?

"There are few things more mysterious than endings."
Salley Vickers

At its outset, near universal unemployment will feel like the dystopian final chapter in the history of American labor. As the end of paid work, it will signal the loss of our occupations, our careers and even our identities; it will dash our hopes and aspirations and toss away our ladders to bigger and better paying jobs. Near universal unemployment won't be just another economic downturn. It will mean the economy itself has turned upside down.

This development will inevitably have a traumatic effect on the American psyche. For a society built on the promise of universal access to a Middle Class (or better) standard of living, the demise of paying jobs will be a dark and fearful development. It will rack us with disappointment and disillusionment, despair and depression. For a culture where success is typically achieved via employment opportunities that, in theory at least, give everyone a legitimate shot at the brass ring, the thought of people being rendered obsolete and unwanted in the workplace will send shivers down our national spine. It will paralyze our native confidence and can-do spirit and convince us that the American Dream is dead.

And yet, there is another way to see this phenomenon. Near universal unemployment also means no more stupid bosses, petty office politics, interminable commutes, 80-hour workweeks for 40-hour salaries, and dangerous, lecherous and boorish co-workers. Near universal unemployment means more personal freedom, less pressure and stress, and the end of workplace injuries, mind-numbing assignments and stock market expectations that push people to cut legal, ethical and environmental corners. And most importantly, escaping the chokehold of paid employment frees us, once and for all, from the biggest con of our time: the phony nirvana of retirement. This Industrial and Information Age Barnumism would have us believe (and accept) that you have to wait until old age to focus on what provides purpose, fulfillment and tranquility in our lives.

From that perspective, near universal unemployment is exactly the opposite of either a dystopia or the end stage of our happiness. It is the gateway to a new American Dream – a reimagination of what we mean when we say we work as long and hard as we do for a single, all-absorbing goal: to create the best possible life for ourselves and a better life for our kids and grandkids.

In the past and even in the present, that idea – that cherished reverie – has been defined in material terms. We work ourselves to the point of exhaustion to be able to afford a nice home, a late model car, food and clothing and a family vacation – the hallmarks of that Middle Class standard of living – and we work harder still so that our children can enjoy an even better version of all that. We dedicate forty or more years of our lives to paid employment so that they might have a more comfortable, safer and healthier life than our own. That has always been the American Dream. And circa 2118, the dream will have come true. Our future families will finally and forever live in a **Tier Two Society**.

THE ADVENT OF
A NEED-FREE NATION

Abraham Maslow famously identified five levels or tiers of human need in his 1943 paper entitled *Hierarchy of Needs: A Theory of Human Motivation*.[25] He named the first or foundational tier Physiological to address humans' basic physical needs – air, water, food, shelter and clothing. He called the second tier Safety to identify their need for personal and financial security as well as health and well-being. In a developed nation such as the United States, most of these needs have been met through paid employment. At least, that's been the case up until now. But in this country and in the not too distant future, that kind of employment will no longer exist. Instead, the United States will have enabled its citizens to meet all of their physical and security needs and to do so without having to work for someone else.

Americans will enjoy the first tier two society in history. Machines will perform all of the labor the country requires for its economy to flourish, and that prosperity will provide an ample standard of living for every person. In 2015, the Pew Research Center found that Middle Class Americans had become a minority, accounting for just 49.9 percent of the country's citizens. Most of the population fell into the Lower Class (29 percent) or the Upper Class (21.1 percent).[26] Circa 2118, that demographic profile will be reversed. The vast majority of Americans will live a stable Middle Class life – one with benefits that far exceed those of today's Middle Class. The Upper Class will comprise a tiny fraction of the population, and the Lower Class – often characterized as the working poor – will cease to exist altogether.

How will this new reality emerge?

Super-C machines will, in fact, free Americans from the dual handcuffs of paid employment and socioeconomic dead ends. However, this new nation will not be some real world Truman Show or a red, white and blue version of Utopia. Humans will remain human, so sadly, there will still be petty antagonisms and bullying, discourtesy and road rage, meanness and character assassinations. Even more disturbing, the country will continue to be plagued by crime and violence, intolerance and bigotry and physical and emotional abuse. It will remain entangled in rhetoric that incites the worst of people and behavior that tramples on people's dignity. And, it will still have to put up with leadership that fails to unite people and ethics that ignore our historic values. All of that will remain a part of the American experience – problems the country must acknowledge and fix – even as its citizens are employment- and want-free … and most especially, because they are.

They will have the full and unfettered opportunity to enjoy a life where all of their physiological and safety needs are met. That salubrious condition will provide both the rationale and the leeway to pursue a new and altogether different goal: the ultimate expression of themselves. They will live in an era when, for the first time in history, everyone will have not one, but two pathways to the summit of their being: they can work at what they do best in an endeavor that fulfills them and they can work at what they hold sacred and infuses them with an enduring tranquility.

On both of those routes, they will employ themselves, not to earn a living, but to elevate their being. They will not work "for" themselves, but will instead work "on" themselves. They won't be 21st century free agents, but rather will act as 22nd century **personal agents**. They will devote themselves to exploring a purpose beyond the traditional markers of a successful life in a modern economy. They will, in short, have the opportunity to work at both their talent and their spirituality.

Americans will enjoy the
first tier two society in history.

Talent has many definitions, of course, but in the world of work, it is best described as something a person loves to do and does especially well. When their talent is applied to their calling – work that they find challenging and meaningful – they earn a deep sense of accomplishment and fulfillment. In contrast, spirituality is defined as "of, relating to, or affecting the human spirit or soul as opposed to material or physical things."[27] When a person's spirituality is applied to a religion or sacred practice – work that they find inspiring and uplifting – they earn a deep sense of inner peace and tranquility.

Together, these two spheres of work are our purpose in being human. Our relationships with family and friends are the gifts of our being, but expressing our talent and spirituality is our individual existential goal. It alone elevates us to a dignity reserved for our species — it alone ennobles us.

No less important, in this new reality of super-C machine domination, that nobility will be an integral feature of the American democracy – it will be achievable by any and everyone. Unlike in earlier times and even in the present, Americans in the 22nd century will be able to devote as much (or as little) of their time as they please to connecting with and exploring their best self and their soul.

Getting to that point, however, will be difficult, even painful for almost everyone. The reality of day-to-day life during the next one hundred years will present a colossal, seemingly insurmountable barrier to the expression of talent and experience of spirituality.

As the opportunity for employment disappears, more and more Americans will lose their financial as well as their physical and emotional support structures. The disruption will be sporadic at first, affecting only those in certain occupations and industries. Then, each passing year will bring the introduction of more and more machines in more and more segments of the economy, until finally, a tipping point will be reached, and the majority of Americans will find themselves out of work and with absolutely no prospect for reemployment.

How will people react? What will the years leading up to 2118 look like? Unfortunately, it isn't hard to imagine what a newsfeed might include...

A frustration-driven tidal wave of citizen anger will crash down on the federal government in general and the Congress in particular. Those in the President's Administration will also get wet, but the more sophisticated and continuous use of social media by its political action committee will convince most people that their local agents – their state's Senators and Representatives – are the real source of the problem. Rallies will be organized on social media and draw hundreds of thousands of people in cities around the country. Many will carry signs that read, *People Are Dreamers. Machines Are Nightmares!*

When Congress still fails to act, protest marches will be held and demonstrators will occupy the local offices of many legislators. The police will intervene when one group of protestors tears down the campaign posters of the Congresswoman from a district in Alabama, and a riot will break out. After the office is cleared two hours later, the manager will find a declaration spray painted in red across the back wall — *Lives matter, not plugs.* It will become yet another rallying cry against machine domination in the workplace.

The misery and accompanying unrest will spread as the weeks pass and soon dwarf that of the Great Depression. Congress will continue to dither, and a 22nd century version of Hoovervilles – called Congresscamps or, more cynically, Concamps for short – will appear in cities around the country. Boston, New York, Atlanta, Chicago, Los Angeles, Portland, Dallas – they will all see Concamps set up in town parks and municipal parking lots. The largest, however, will be in Washington, D.C. where it will cover every square inch of ground on both sides of the Lincoln Memorial Reflecting Pool. One old-timer will tell the press that it reminds him of the throngs he witnessed when Martin Luther King, Jr. delivered his "I Have a Dream" speech on the same spot. Only this time, he'll add, it's not the color of our skin that's the problem but the capacity of our brain.

These communities of protest will keep up a daily barrage of demands aimed at the Congress. Members of both the House and Senate will convene emergency committee hearings and meet in rump sessions. They will conduct debates in their respective chambers and opine in front of the microphones at press conferences. They will devote thousands of hours to talking about the crisis, and in the end, produce nothing more than a mélange of band-aid solutions. These bills will have august sounding names – the most notable being The Defense of Individual Prosperity, Commercial Strength and National Vigor Act – but none will have the funding or the priority to redress the situation. They will be ridiculed on late night TV shows as "Con games" and reviled in the Concamps as a waste of time.

Finally, with the prospect of violence growing more and more real and the Congress unable to devise an appropriate solution, the Administration will propose a sweeping program to reset the social and economic structure of the country. Unlike the New Deal programs during the Great Depression, this initiative will not be envisioned as a bridge over troubled times – a sanctuary for citizens until the economy recovers. Rather, it will place the country on a road that leads to an entirely new destination. It will both acknowledge that the economy will never return to what it once was – a platform for employment-for-fee work – and provide a way for the country to establish a breathtaking new reality – a platform for employment-for-free work.

The legislation will initially face fierce opposition from the fearful and the deniers in both parties in the Congress. They will argue that the bill is too sweeping, too radical and pushes the country too far into a future with too many unknowns. They will use procedural tactics to delay committee votes and call in favors to try and attach poison pill amendments. Their opposition will briefly hold up the bill's consideration and then collapse in the face of a super storm of public protest.

Email and old-fashioned letters will flood into Congressional offices by the millions. Phone systems will freeze up in the face of an unprecedented volume of constituent calls. And, newspapers will enjoy an economic revival as they print daily, full-page ads paid for by advocacy groups that all have the same message: #*PassItNow*. Six weeks later, the Congress will do just that, and the United States will establish the first-ever fully Government subsidized Universal Health Insurance (UHI) and Universal Basic Income (UBI) program for its citizens.

THE RISE OF AN OMNI CLASS

No sooner will the UHI/UBI legislation pass than the questions will begin. Not surprisingly, the first will be about taxes. Despite claims by the Administration that the new program "will let you keep all your money," Americans will quickly discover that they can (and will) be taxed at both the state and federal level. While the UBI, itself, will not be subject to taxation, any additional income a person earns will be. Americans will still be free to make as much money as they want or can to supplement their federal paycheck. They will still be able to launch new businesses, make investments and even accept employment with and for others, but they will pay tax on any wealth they accumulate over and above their UBI.

The introduction of this healthcare and income support program will reset America's sense of itself as "the land of opportunity." American citizens in the 22nd century will simply not understand the need for employment to pay for basic necessities or to cover the cost of a visit to the doctor. Their history books will describe a time in the 21st century when formerly successful workers lived in their cars after being laid off or had to file for bankruptcy after a prolonged illness. They will read about working parents who could not afford school supplies or healthy meals for their kids and see pictures of toddlers playing in a filthy backyard with a sign on the fence reading Only Smiles Day Care. They'll be taught all about what their parents and grandparents experienced, but to them it will be a foreign and incomprehensible America.

All of their living requirements will be met through their guaranteed access to a new Middle Class, one that is so broadly representative of the population, it will be renamed the **Omni Class**. Equally as important, every American will enjoy the standard of living consistent with that class. They will have the same income and the same medical, dental and psychological care as everyone else, and they will have those resources for life. Industrial and Information Age divisions – the Lower and Middle Classes – will no longer be relevant, as more than 99 percent of the population will be designated by a single classification that eliminates any distinction based on paycheck or quality of life.

Despite the warnings of those who oppose such a move – called MickeyCs in a tip of the hat to a former Wisconsin Senator – the resulting economy will not be a version of communism, where in theory, at least, all economic goods are owned by the people and allocated according to their need. Nor will it be a form of socialism and transfer the means of production to the people. The private sector will not only still exist circa 2118, it will flourish thanks to the hard work of super-C machines and the tireless spending of American consumers.

Indeed, the introduction of a universal basic income will launch a business-friendly phenomenon in the country known as the **upgrade economy**. Each year, a large segment of the American population will purchase a new model of several key possessions – their computers, phones, clothing, footwear, eyeglasses and watches, to name just a few – and that drive to have the latest and greatest will fuel strong corporate growth. Companies will stop identifying each new generation of their products with a sequential number – aphone 7, aphone 8 or 9 – and instead differentiate them by year – aphone 20 in 2120, aphone 21 in 2121 and so on. Each year, they will crank out a new and more alluring version, and each year, consumers will grab them up. Bottom lines will bulge, but so too will city and town landfills.

Americans' discarded possessions will quickly overwhelm local capacity and an environmental crisis will erupt. Entrepreneurs will sense an opportunity, and in short order, commercial launch companies will begin offering economical space dumping for municipalities in need of an alternative to traditional earthbound sites. A visible ring of human debris will then begin to grow in the sky, provoking an intense response from environmental groups. Their lobbying will ultimately succeed, and Congress will pass a law prohibiting such activity. Called the NMT or No More Teslas Act, it will ban the junking of private possessions in or above the Earth's atmosphere. While it will be effective in halting such activity among legitimate businesses, however, it will not prevent a resilient capitalism from establishing a new "dark space market of hi-dumpers."

All of their living requirements will be met through their guaranteed access to a new Middle Class, one that is so broadly representative of the population, it will be renamed the Omni Class.

America's much revered rugged individualism will be similarly resilient, despite its citizens almost universal membership in the Omni Class. They will be neither clones of one another nor faceless denizens of some latter day proletariat. In fact, the one attribute they will share is their access to the first true freedom of expression on the planet. Even more so than today, they will each be able to distinguish themselves through the products they choose to purchase and the services they decide to use. In addition, the range of options from which they can select – whether it's the car they drive, the clothes they wear, the vacations they take or the entertainment they enjoy – and the caliber of the options they can afford will be vastly greater than ever before.

More importantly, every individual will also have the independence to "work" at something that elevates their life to a fuller and richer experience and thereby ennobles them. Their income will not be unlimited, of course, but its very universality will ensure that each and every "jobless American" will have an equal opportunity for self-exploration and expression. They will be free to participate in whatever pursuit – social, civic, religious, metaphysical, cultural or athletic – they believe will empower them to achieve a more vibrant and enduring connection with both the substance of their life and whatever they accept as sacred and divine. They will, in effect, be able to step off into an entirely new era of individual purpose.

PAYING THE BILL

As expensive as a Tier Two Society with a huge Omni Class will be, it will enjoy a strong and durable financial foundation that makes it eminently feasible. That foundation will be very different from the one used to support today's entitlement programs. The current social security net – which helps to keep people out of poverty and in good health – is widely acknowledged to be unsustainable because it taxes fewer and fewer employed and amply compensated workers to pay for the benefits received by more and more no longer employed and financially dependent workers.

The UHI/UBI program, in contrast, will be a **social prosperity net** – it will support the workers in a tier two society, but its financial foundation will not incur a debt their children and grandchildren will have to pay. It will not bankrupt the future to finance the present. Instead, funding for the UHI/UBI program will be generated by two new taxes that spare the average American:

- a tax on the point-1 percent of the population whose income significantly exceeds the UBI;

and

- a tax on the organizations that employ machines to do the work formerly done by humans.

THE OMNI CLASS
PROTECTION TAX

This tax on wealthy Americans will be viewed as both a mechanism for partially funding the UHI/ UBI program and a way to counter the emergence of a quasi-oligarchical class in 21st century American society. The individuals in that class will have gained a dangerous level of power through their ability to influence political parties, social and political commentators, and the media as well as government officials, regulatory agencies and even the judiciary. As it was with the robber barons of the early Industrial Age, the source of their power will be their wealth. Some will have amassed their money through investments and advantageous tax treatments, and others will have stuffed their pockets while working as an executive in a public company.

According to the Economic Policy Institute, the average pay of a corporate CEO (including the stock options they cash in as well as their salary, bonuses, restricted stock grants and long-term incentive payouts) was a walloping 271 times greater than the average pay of a typical worker in 2017.[28] That disparity will continue to grow until, circa 2118, it will be seen as a threat to both the wellbeing of the American democracy and to the perceived fairness and, ultimately, the legitimacy of the Universal Basic Income. The Omni Class Protection Tax will be imposed as a way of redressing it.

This new version of the alternative minimum

tax will be triggered any time an individual's or family's income is 20 or more times greater than the UBI, regardless of whether that income was earned via investments, carried interest or as executive compensation. That 20-to-1 ratio will be chosen because it was the difference between the average pay of CEOs and that of workers in 1965.[29] In many respects, that year was just like the one before it and, at least for awhile, the ones after it, as well. But, it was also a year when the Middle Class still existed in America, and a Middle Class paycheck still provided a respectable standard of living and still supported a credible American Dream. No less important, it was a time when almost everyone could aspire to join that Middle Class, and the Omni Class Protection Tax will, in part, subsidize a return to such universal opportunity.

THE MACHINE EMPLOYMENT TAX

A new tax on businesses is never popular with the private sector. Well, almost never. Circa 2118, corporate executives and business owners in every segment of the economy and in transnational corporations as well as small and mid-sized companies will support a tax on the organizations that employ machines to do the work humans had previously done. It won't be the position of everyone, of course, but it will be that of most business leaders.

They will cite four reasons for taking this uncharacteristic position:

- First, this so-called "labor replacement tax" will actually save them money. It will cost their businesses less than what they were previously spending on human workers for their pay, healthcare insurance and other benefits, federal and state regulatory filings and other fees, morale building activities, and the not-so-hidden expense of having to recruit a replacement when an employee decides to depart.

- Second, in the early years of the super-C machine era – when these systems will take on many but not all jobs – companies will also be able to significantly reduce the overhead costs associated with a human workforce. These reductions will be made in Finance and Accounting, IT, Procurement and Legal Affairs as well as in the Human Resource Department. Some of the positions in these areas will, themselves, be automated, while others will no longer be necessary as the workforce shrinks.

The HR Department, however, will be an anomaly. As machines take over human jobs, fewer and fewer of its staff will be needed for such traditional functions as record keeping and compliance, compensation and benefits administration, labor relations, performance management, training and development and recruitment. On the other hand, at least some of the Department's staff will be required to implement the organization's reduction-in-(human) force and to ensure the layoffs are executed in accordance with all state and federal regulations and in as compassionate and supportive a way as possible. In many companies, therefore, HR professionals will be among the first to go and also among the last.

• Third, the new tax will be defined by the accounting profession as a legitimate cost of doing business and treated by the states and the federal government as an appropriate deduction under their tax codes. Instead of hurting their market competitiveness, therefore, the tax will actually be a boon to companies at the bottom line.

• Fourth and most importantly, the business leaders of the time will quickly realize that the economy in general and their companies in particular will quickly sputter to a halt without the holiday, birthday, anniversary, vacation, entertainment, household, automotive and just plain day-to-day spending of the Great American Consumer. A consumer-based economy needs consumer spending, so if Americans can no longer earn the money to play that role through employment, they must receive it from the government in the form of a guarantee subsidized by businesses themselves.

These two taxes will solidify and support the new reality of a Tier Two Society in America. They will ensure that every single American has the genuine opportunity to pursue Happiness in any way they want … except through a paying job.

Chapter 4

What Will
Humans Do?

*"Oh, you hate your job? Why didn't you say
so? There's a support group for that. It's called
everybody, and they meet at the bar."*
Drew Carey

The rise of the byte-collar workforce and the resulting phenomenon of near universal unemployment will confront American workers with an unsettling paradox. What should be a catastrophe will also feel like a blessing. What should evoke desperation and despair will actually elicit unbridled joy. The country's workers will find themselves thrown out of jobs they need and sometimes even value and, at the same time, exult in their freedom from having to work in those jobs.

From the dawn of the Industrial Age and through the entirety of the Information Age, parents and teachers, therapists and life coaches counseled working men and women to put employment in perspective. It is not, they advised, the end-all and be-all of one's life. It is not something that should infringe on our relationships or determine our self-image. And, to drive that point home, they often concluded with the admonition that no one has ever had their tombstone inscribed with the phrase:

"I wish I had spent more time in the office."

The vast majority of Americans would probably agree with that sentiment, yet in the present at least, they spend most of their lives on-the-job. They're in the office, on the plant floor and on the road so much they miss their kids' soccer matches, their spouses' birthdays and their parents' anniversaries. They obsess about their jobs when they're at home, often pacing the floor on sleepless nights and stealing time away from weekends to call a coworker. And, they take those jobs with them on their vacations, walking the beach early in the morning or holding back on a hike to check their email. Americans have become the always-on workers, toiling away at their jobs even when they're not actually in the workplace.

THE GUT PUNCH OF MODERN-DAY WORK

Why do we throw ourselves into work we think

so little of that we don't want to be remembered for it? Why do we spend so much time on and at our jobs if we hold them in such low regard?

The obvious answer, of course, is that we need to earn a living. We have to satisfy those tier one and tier two needs in Maslow's hierarchy. Until we win the lottery or get word of a huge inheritance from a previously unknown aunt, there's no other way to acquire the "basic necessities," let alone reward ourselves with an occasional (or more frequent) splurge. So, holding your nose while holding down a job is ... well, it's just part of being an adult. Like sagging chins and tiring early, it comes with the territory. That's what most of us tell ourselves, and yet, sociologists believe there's more going on.

They say that, at least for some, it is the fear of being seen as unnecessary or unreliable by employers that no longer show any loyalty at all to their employees.

If you're out of the office, you're in danger of being out of a job.

Other experts argue that, in an overscheduled and stress-filled culture, it's a marginally better alternative to home life and all of its familial obligations.

At least in the office, you don't feel guilty when you can't be super-parent or super-spouse.

And, still others opine that working provides an accessible if imperfect platform for one of humankind's most powerful urges: the drive to do something well and worthwhile.

You endure tiring commutes and depressing cubicle swamps because you're determined to be the best you can be each day.

Given the variability of human life, there's undoubtedly a measure of truth in all of those views. They are not, however, the root cause of our clear commitment to something so many of us find so unpleasant. That original source is a societal mental disorder. We Americans suffer from **work-related cognitive dissonance**. Yes, to be sure, that's a gross generalization. And certainly, there are some who love what they do and enjoy every minute they spend on-the-job. But they are the rarest of exceptions to the general rule.

As a browser search for the term "how to find meaning in your work" makes clear, most of us would never, ever voluntarily spend more time in the office or on the plant floor. In August of 2017, for example, that inquiry yielded 1,370,000,000 results; a month later, there were even more. We are desperate to find something, anything that will transform our job into an endeavor worthy of our best effort. Employers describe work as an "employment opportunity;" everyone else on the planet sees it as a four-letter word. It yokes us to a daily grind that fails to engage or fulfill us, even as we are compelled to spend most of our waking day immersed in it.

That is cognitive dissonance. Wikipedia defines the condition as "the mental discomfort (psychological stress) experienced by a person who simultaneously holds two or more contradictory beliefs, ideas, or values."[30] In other words, American workers endure the distastefulness of devoting themselves to jobs they can barely tolerate because they hold two contradictory views of the work they do in those jobs.

On the one hand, many of us define ourselves by our occupation – by the role we have chosen and the kind of work we have been trained to perform. When asked what we do, we say we are a sales manager or an HR professional, an engineer or a teacher. We are proud of our career field and our expertise in it. When we are able to express that competence – when we are challenged in work that taps its fullest measure and achieves goals we consider meaningful – we feel as if we've done something worthwhile with our day. We earn a sense of satisfaction and something deeper – fulfillment – from that outcome and the contribution it enables us to make to our team, the organization or both.

On the other hand, our employment experience – the jobs we are paid to do in the organizations that pay us to do them – are frequently devoid of that kind of work. And even if the work is meaningful, we are constrained by office politics, incompetent and biased bosses, rapaciously greedy and self-serving executives and outdated or nonexistent technology from being able to do that work as it should be done. We arrive at our jobs each day to have some of our best moments, and exactly the opposite happens. From the minute we walk through the door, we feel nothing but disillusion and discouragement and the insult of an ever-shrinking paycheck.

That's why none of us ever wish we had spent more time in the office, and yet, each week we do. Hope springs eternal ... and so too do our grocery bills.

THE GREAT TALENT ROBBERY

This work-related cognitive dissonance has been made even worse by the Great Talent Robbery of the 20th and early 21st centuries. This heist was perpetrated by elementary and high school administrators and by the faculties of undergraduate and graduate programs in our colleges and universities. They've convinced generations of Americans that talent is something reserved for only a precious few in the population. They've brainwashed kids and their parents into accepting that those who are the most capable physically – think professional athletes; creatively – think musicians and actors; and intellectually – think Westinghouse Science Talent Search winners, are the only ones in our species endowed with talent. They've led everyone else to believe that they were at the end of the line when talent was handed out.

The Gifted and Talented programs administered in elementary schools across the nation are a perfect case in point. Based on an arbitrarily determined intelligence quotient (IQ) score, they recognize a select group of kids as "gifted and talented," which by definition means that every other child was born without a gift or talent. They take care of the kids who are – at least according to the standard of these experts – intellectually superior and consign the rest of the kids to a standardized education that views and treats them as an average Joe or Jane student. As devoted as their teachers may be, that experience all too often leads these youngsters to conclude that they have nothing special to offer. They accept their designation and shape their performance according-ly. They become average Joe and Jane graduates.

And, that's a tragedy. Because these "average" Joe and Jane graduates become average Joe and Jane adults. They go through life believing that they have no talent and therefore cannot be extraor-dinary, cannot excel at something that inspires and fulfills them. Average Joe and Jane adults become average Joe and Jane workers and average Joe and Jane citizens. While some will be able to break out of this Manchurian mindlock, many won't. They will be able to soar – they will have the capacity to achieve superior performance in an endeavor they consider important – but they will spend their en-tire life mislead into mediocrity, boredom or both.

What they won't realize, what they will never dis-cover is that talent is not defined by an IQ score. Or by how sweetly they can sing. Or by how far they can throw a football. It is not limited to their abil-ity to wow the judges in some contest. Or to their interest in discovering a new strain of bacteria. No, talent is the opposite of all that. It is not a gift bestowed only on an elite few, but instead, is a far more encompassing attribute with a much greater reach.

Talent is the **capacity for excellence**, and it resides in each and all of us. It is an attribute of our species. Like our opposable thumb, talent is one of the characteristics that defines being human. Everyone has it, waiting to be discovered inside them. It is a universal trait that is expressed in far more ways than the ability to do well on science projects and the basketball court. It can be the ability to communicate complex ideas clearly in speech or prose. Or the ability to organize a diverse group and lead them in the accomplishment of a specific task. Or the ability to show compassion and care for those in need. Talent can be all of those genuine and special competencies, and every single one of them can be put to work, even in today's high tech economy.

We go to work to have some of our best moments and, instead, are thrown into a pit of frustration, disillusion and discouragement as well as the insult of an ever-shrinking paycheck.

The Great Talent Robbery, therefore, has impoverished America in two ways. First, it has created a workforce filled with undiscovered and therefore unemployed talent. These individual capacities to excel can be married to a grounding in STEM – the subjects of science, technology, engineering and mathematics – and bring excellence to high tech enterprises. They can also be applied in settings that do not involve or require such a grounding and deliver excellence there, as well.

Talent is a mission critical asset for all employers, and one they struggle to find in today's workforce. Not because it doesn't exist – there is no talent shortage in America – but because it is hidden away within the country's working men and women. Employers can't access it because workers don't even know it's there. Most have never been given permission to look for it or taught how to recognize and nurture it. As a result, America is a nation rich in talent, but its employers are talent poor, undermining their performance and their competitive position in the global marketplace.

The second way in which the Great Talent Robbery has impoverished America is by its denial of a fundamental individual right. The capacity for excellence is not only something that all Americans have, it is an aspect of life they all deserve to experience.

The Declaration of Independence states that people have been endowed with certain unalienable rights, and though not enumerated by the Founding Fathers, the expression of their talent is certainly one of them. They have that right because doing something worthwhile with the best of themselves is the only sure way they can reach for Happiness. And as with Life and Liberty, the pursuit of Happiness is an enumerated right. So, the abnegation of talent among all those average Joes or Janes cancels out their ability to excel and that, in turn, denies them access to their potential pinnacle of success in the workplace. They never get to experience their talent or to enjoy the Happiness its expression can bring.

This Great Talent Robbery together with work-related cognitive dissonance will shape the paradox caused by the rise of super-C machines and near universal unemployment in America. As the nation's workers deal with that situation, however, as they try to make sense of how it will affect and change them, they will be thrust into even more uncertainties. To riff on a phrase first used by Winston Churchill, they will find themselves dealing with a paradox wrapped around a question encased in a mystery. They will both exult in and fear the loss of work to super-C machines even as they ask themselves what there is left for them to do with their lives while they search for purpose in a world where they are no longer the smartest creation. They will teeter on the edge of more unknowns than they have ever had to face.

THE NEONAISSANCE:
THE BIRTH OF
SELF-ENNOBLEMENT

Circa 2118, super-C machines will be an accepted part of the American experience. There will be no debate about their role as they will significantly improve the quality of life for most people. There will be no handwringing about controlling them as they will have been fully and effectively integrated into our economy and society. Those of us alive today will, of course, have to struggle with the unemployment they cause – our careers will be shaped and eventually distorted by it – but our kids and grandkids will have a very different challenge. They will live in a world where machines exceed human capabilities in almost every field and fill human jobs in almost every corner of the workplace. The test of their generations, therefore, will be to answer a single question. *What can and should humans do?*

This dilemma will not be an existential crisis – it won't threaten the continuity of our species – but it will be one that strikes at the very essence of being human. While science fiction has long imagined a future of hostile machines determined to enslave humankind, a more likely scenario – indeed, the one that is already unfolding in America – is the silent spring of human workers in the traditional workplace.

Near universal unemployment is certainly less violent than an attack by Terminators, but it is just as threatening to our status on the planet and frighteningly more realistic. It establishes an economy turned upside down – a world of work in which humans are no longer the supreme architects of commercial success or even a valued resource in organizations. We will go from being indispensable to inconsequential, from being employed to being eliminated.

Thanks to the UBI, we will still have an income, but it will leave us wanting and unsatisfied in another way. We will have all of the tier one and two support we need, yet lack the sense of accomplishment that can come from earning it. We will be dignity poor. Even worse, without gainful employment, we will have nothing to build our dreams on, nothing that will infuse our days with challenge and give them meaning. Super-C machines will establish a workplace that can – and will – get along very well without us. They won't be our masters; they will be our occupational end stage. They won't terminate our lives; they will terminate our access to purpose in life.

This dark assessment will almost certainly be the way many Americans view the rise of super-C machines. These code-based creations may not blast us with their hyper-cannons, but they will cripple us just the same. And to be fair, there's certainly a logic to such a conclusion – after all, we will have lost a core element of human life since at least the Middle Ages. We will no longer be able to feel the sense of satisfaction and self-esteem that comes from having been employed to do useful work.

The temp staffing firm owner turned faux President in the movie *Dave* described it this way:

> "If you've ever seen the look on
> somebody's face the day they finally get
> a job, I've had some experience with this,
> they look like they could fly. And it's not
> about the paycheck, it's about respect, it's

about looking in the mirror and knowing that you've done something valuable with your day."

Losing the ability to achieve that sense of a day well spent will traumatize many, maybe even most American workers. It will call into question their worth as a person and their value as a contributing member of society. It will shake their self-confidence and undermine their self-esteem. For men and women raised to see themselves as independent and capable wage earners – whether that wage is an hourly paycheck or a salary in six figures – being unable to play that role will cast them as useless or, worse, as losers in society.

This perspective, however, has an inherent flaw. It is based on a single and heretofore unchallenged assumption. Though seldom explicitly stated, this foundational notion is the only rationale for seeing the rise of byte-collar workers as something to be feared. It accepts that there is nothing a machine can't do and do infinitely better than humans. It concedes that machines will be programmed and then learn on their own to think, act, intuit, react, and even empathize more perfectly than people. Feeling threatened by machine-based unemployment makes perfect sense, if you assume that machines can and will out-human humans in every facet of being human.

And, that assumption is wrong. It is too simple, too sweeping, too black and white to be credible. Life – and especially human life – is much more complex and dynamic than an all-or-nothing – a 1 or 0 – outcome. And it's that complexity which ensures a fulsome future for humankind.

It is true that machines will ultimately achieve superiority over humans in every aspect of human cognition and creativity. That outcome doesn't diminish humans, however, it opens them to becoming something better. When machines take on all of the trials and tribulations, all of the burdens and chores, all of the obligations and to-dos of day-to-day living, humans will acquire the freedom to examine and enhance their lives. When machines are harnessed to the daily grind of employment, humans will finally be able to work on themselves. To discover and express their unique capacity for excellence and to search for answers to questions beyond the comprehension of even the most intelligent machine. To reach for the nobility of being human.

Such work befuddles even super-C machines. They cannot be programmed or learn by themselves to calculate, reason or infer their own nobility. It is not a matter of the state-of-the-art – in the next 100 years or in the next millennium – it is a matter of what is possible. And, it is impossible for a machine to probe its life or its soul. It has neither.

Humans can transfer their intelligence to a machine. They may eventually transfer even their sensitivity and empathy. But what they cannot do, what they don't have the power to do, is to give machines a life or a soul. Life is a condition which incorporates "the capacity for growth, reproduction, functional activity, and continual change," which, at work, is expressed as talent.[31] The soul, in contrast, is sometimes described as the "incorporeal essence" of a person's being, which is experienced through their spirituality.[32]

These two features are an irreducible part of who humans are, so they have access to them, but they cannot replicate or even approximate them. In fact, for most humans, their life and their soul are the two greatest and most profound mysteries they will confront during their time on Earth. The best they can ever hope to do, therefore, is to explore them. And yet, that very ability – that faculty for venturing deep within themselves in search of their own talent and spirituality – is an extraordinary grant. It is the one facility with which all humankind and humankind alone has been endowed.

A pessimistic view of the rise of super-C machines is based on the assumption that machines can and will out-human humans in every facet of being human.

This loophole in human fate will establish a new and more perfect era in American history. When 2118 dawns, super-C machines will do what they do best, and as a consequence, free up humans to do that which only they can do. Super-C machines will take over all blue, white, gray, pink, rainbow and no-collar jobs, so our grandkids and great grandkids can work on getting in touch with and better comprehending both their own lives and their souls. They will live and labor and rejoice in an era known as the **Neonaissance** (neon ais sance).

The establishment of the UHI/UBI will make this quest for existential purpose possible and give it a singular character. In one respect, of course, the journey is hardly new – humans have been talented and spiritual beings since their earliest days on the planet. What is unique about this pilgrimage, however, is its common vernacular. It will speak to all Americans, regardless of their background, their physical or intellectual gifts or their social standing. Exploring these mysteries, then, will be a modern-day version of Chaucer's *Canterbury Tales*. It will be a journey open to all and shaped by their individual discoveries.

Maslow called the need to express our talent – our innate capacity for excellence – "self-actualization." It is an elusive concept for many thanks to the Great Talent Robbery, and yet, it is a pinnacle of performance to which many if not most of us instinctively aspire. The entrepreneur and investor David Sze described it this way: "Self-actualization occurs when you maximize your potential, doing the best that you are capable of doing."[33] When people are liberated from organizational, societal and other barriers – when they are able to work at something they enjoy and find meaningful – they are inherently motivated to perform at their peak.

The need to express our spirituality, on the other hand, is more widely recognized, if less well understood. Maslow, himself, didn't comprehend the power of the need until very late in life, at which point, he amended his hierarchy to include it as the ultimate tier called "self-transcendence." The scholar Mark E. Koltko-Rivera described it as work where people "seek communion with the transcendent, perhaps through mystical or transpersonal experiences; [and in doing so] they come to identify with something greater than the purely individual self...."[34] When people are liberated from the physical requirements of their existence – when they have food, clothing, shelter, health and security – they are motivated to explore the metaphysical questions only humans can answer.

Fundamentally, the Neonaissance is an historic opportunity to leverage the benefits of a Tier Two Society in order to address both these uniquely human needs at the very apex of what drives us and ultimately distinguishes us as a species. It will enable all Americans to recognize and realize the purpose of being human: to elevate themselves to the singular nobility of their species. To reach for and assume their inherent dignity and exceptionalism.

For many, the advent of this new era will be hard to believe or accept. Some will criticize it as New Age mumbo-jumbo, while others will mock its lack of quantifiable measures of definition. Some will revel in machine fear-mongering and castigate the era's positive view of byte-collar ascendance as an adult fairy tale (or nightmare). And, still others will snark that humans will inevitably create machines in their own image, so we are more likely to see automated indifference, intolerance and even cruelty than some touchy-feely pathway to higher living.

These negative reactions, however, will not change the facts. In the absence of physical and safety needs and with all conventional and essential work being done by machines, humans will – for the first time in their history – have the freedom to do whatever they wish. While some will fritter away their liberation, many – and hopefully most – will see it as a human right they must respect and a human responsibility they must honor. It creates the opportunity to experience the fulfillment that comes from expressing the best aspects of our life and the tranquility only a connection with our soul can offer.

Those two outcomes are worthy of our best efforts in their own right, but together, they provide an additional and equally important benefit: they establish the continued superiority of our species on the planet. They enable humans to be greater than machines. Those technological creations will out-perform humans on-the-job, but humans will out-perfect machines as beings.

The Neonaissance will begin in America, therefore, not only because of the nation's technological superiority, but because its animating dynamic is the ultimate and truest expression of American democratic participation. It is the enactment of Liberty and the pursuit of Happiness, to be sure, but equally as important, it is the celebration of Life itself. It is the perfection of those Rights with which they have been endowed by their Creator.

To reach that state, however – to realize the Age of Ennoblement – Americans will first have to endure the next one hundred years. They will have to overcome the challenges of a Second Middle Ages.

Chapter 5

The Second Middle Ages (MA2)

"My fate is to live among varied and confusing storms. But for you perhaps, if as I hope and wish you will live long after me, there will be a better age.... When the darkness has been dispersed, our descendants can come again in the former pure radiance."

Petrarch, *Africa*

To reach the Age of Ennoblement, Americans will first have to address and resolve a crisis of individual and societal disruption unlike any ever faced by their nation. They will have to contend with machine domination in more and more segments of the economy and with the diminution of human employment opportunities that is its result.

Inherently an optimistic tribe, many Americans will find such a forecast difficult to accept, especially during the next year or two. The evidence, at least as measured in traditional economic and business metrics, seems to paint a very different and much more positive picture. Andrew Sullivan put it this way in *New York Magazine* in January, 2018:

> "Economic growth is now ubiquitous in the developed world (including even Japan) for the first time in quite a while. In America, we are in a record eighth year of economic growth, bringing peak employment and finally a bump in earnings. Median household income is now the highest in history ... Global conflict continues its long centuries-old decline. ISIS has been destroyed in its own heartland. Anyone with a phone has access to more learning and knowledge than at any point in human history. More people live in democracies today than a dozen years ago. When natural disasters happen, they kill fewer people in a far more populous world. The last decade has seen the biggest decline in global poverty ever."[35]

And yet, beneath the surface patina of these positive indicators, there is trouble stirring. Yes, life today is pretty good, regardless of how you feel about the country's leaders, role models and cultural icons. People are working, business is booming, and the

American economy is still the mightiest on Earth. That's good news, to be sure, but it doesn't eliminate the danger. Nor can it prepare us for it. Even the sure knowledge that every economic upturn is always eventually followed by a downturn is no safe haven. Every American in the workforce understands and, to some extent, expects to experience these cycles of business and employment. What they haven't experienced before – what they are now about to confront – is a new compass heading that will bring the good times to a halt and open a fundamentally different and much more disturbing reality in its place.

*To reach the Age of Ennoblement,
Americans will first have to
address and resolve a crisis
of individual and societal
disruption unlike any ever faced
by their nation.*

This transformative period will bring American's subliminal uneasiness with ever more powerful and capable machines out into the open where it will fester and metastasize. Over the next one hundred years, they will watch helplessly as humans are toppled from their perch at the top of the evolutionary stack and can no longer claim to be the most capable creatures on the planet. The evidence will be too pervasive, the changes too omnipresent for people to ignore. They will be forced to acknowledge that machines can out-think, outwork, outlast and outdo them in every facet of what used to be called "human endeavor."

This realization will hit them first as a nagging worry in the dead of night and then as a seeping desperation during their waking day. What has always been clear and well understood will become inscrutable. What has always been reliable will become doubtful or worse, unknowable. And what has always been a source of security will suddenly become precarious and even threatening.

THE GREATNESS TO COME

The coming economic, political, cultural and individual disruption will stagger every American's understanding of the present and batter their confidence in the future. It will leave them groggy with confusion and self-doubt. It will stir anger and numbness, aggression and withdrawal, desperation and defiance, all at the same time. It will be a stern test of America's mettle, its spirit, and its determination to measure up to its principles and self-image.

The next one hundred years will be a challenge every bit as severe and momentous as the cataclysm of World War II. That epic struggle is considered one of America's gravest crises and most heroic victories, so undoubtedly, there are some who will call such a comparison overstated, if not entirely inappropriate. In truth, it is not. The threat posed by super-C machines is no less potentially catastrophic to the integrity of America – to its values, its vision and its quality of life – than the militarism of Nazi Germany and the Empire of Japan. America's response, therefore, must be commensurate, as well, to that of those who fought and won that historic conflict.

Those young Americans have been called "the greatest generation." And, with good reason. They defeated a global assault on democracy and the human values it celebrates and nurtures. They prevailed in the face of desperate missions and horrific conditions, and in doing so, they were heroic and deserving of the nation's recognition.

Most, however, would disavow any claim to being the greatest. Old soldiers are a modest legion, and they would likely say the adjective goes too far. The word suggests that they were the ultimate expression of American character – after all, there can be nothing greater than the greatest. And, that's the very antithesis of what they believed in and fought for.

In World War II, America's men went into combat and America's women nursed their wounds and built the arsenal of democracy for one reason: to preserve and protect the future. They were great so their children could be greater than they were and their grandchildren greater still. They didn't aspire to be the ultimate pinnacle of American resolve and courage, but rather to be the foundation on which the pinnacle could be raised even further.

That legacy will fortify the American people for the next one hundred years. This period will also try and test the nation, but it too will fall short of overwhelming or defeating us. The rise of super-C machines will not count us out or put us down. Eventually, we – the generations of today's America – will confront the challenge of machine hegemony in the workplace, and we will measure up to it. We will accept our call to greatness. We will stand up in front of this new reality – we will look this powerful technology squarely in the eye – and we will do whatever is necessary to become the master of its changes rather than their victim.

To do that, however, we must first refocus our view of today's world of work. We must actually see this new era – we must recognize it as a real and present danger – and acknowledge the threat it poses to us and those we hold dear. Only then will we hear our call to greatness and muster the resolve to meet the challenge successfully.

The disruption caused by super-C machines to date has been so sporadic, so hit-or-miss that it hasn't risen to the level of general consciousness. For most people, the impact of these machines is something they read about in magazines or blog posts or hear about on television or podcasts, but it's not a factor in their own lives. It may have thrown a neighbor out of work or even a distant relative, but it hasn't touched their own job or disrupted their own family.

As a result, people are aware of technology's growing presence in the workplace, but only in a superficial and unconnected way. Indeed, a 2017 survey of 2,773 adult Americans found that fewer than one-in-ten (just 7 percent) were worried about the impact of super-C machine technology on their employment prospects. Almost half (41 percent) admitted that they didn't know whether it would amount to anything that could or would affect their lives. Even the most tech savvy generation in American history – those now in college – were sanguine about the role of technology in their careers. Better than seven-out-of-ten (71 percent) said they either hardly thought about it or didn't think about it at all when deciding which occupational field to pursue.[36]

CORRECTING THE MYOPIA

The best way to correct this societal myopia – the only way to mobilize the next Great Generations of Americans – is to turn once again to history. As the passage between a familiar past and a transformative future, this period is comparable to the Middle Ages, the passage that led to the Renaissance. In fact, the similarities are so pronounced that the earlier period should now be called the First Middle Ages because the next one hundred years will be a Second.

The two eras denote extraordinarily difficult times for the general population – the first in Europe, the second in the United States. In the First Middle Ages (MA1), Europe experienced political upheaval, feudalism, warfare and the triple diseases of the Black Plague. While trade flourished and universities were founded, the majority of working people led a hard life that either indentured them to an overlord or left them teetering on the edge of starvation.[37] In the Second Middle Ages (MA2), the United States will endure political unrest, mass unemployment, societal friction and the constant threat of terrorism. While the stock market will soar and healthcare will improve, middle class workers will see their careers decimated and their quality of life eviscerated as technology pushes them out of the workplace and into financial distress. The First Middle Ages is sometimes described as the Dark Ages; the Second Middle Ages will come to be known as the Inflamed Ages.

We will stand up in front of this new reality - we will look this powerful technology squarely in the eye - and we will do whatever is necessary to become the master of its changes rather than their victim.

It is a comparison of the architecture of these two periods, however, that provides the greatest clarity. The First Middle Ages was a bridge between the art, science and philosophy of the Roman Empire and its rebirth in Europe in the Renaissance. It was an interval between two times that had similar roots, so while their artistic and scholarly expressions were very different, their foundations were composed of the same intellectual material.

The Second Middle Ages, in contrast, will be a fundamental and permanent departure from the past. It will reset the rationalism, empiricism, and analysis of the Industrial and Information Ages as important but no longer the preeminent features of human endeavor and pair them with aspirational drives that encourage and enable self-ennoblement. The net effect of the First Middle Ages was a continuity in perspective and thought. The net effect of the Second will be a discontinuity – a fracture in human priorities and purpose.

This rupture will not occur as a big bang – as a sudden or explosive event. It will not be the lead story on cable news for a night or two only to disappear when some other cultural happening of equal magnitude blasts into our lives. And, it will not trend on social media for 15 minutes and then be displaced as something else even more quirky creeps into our lives on little cat feet. No, this century-long separation from all we have ever known will impose itself on our consciousness as a clammy blanket we can't shrug off. It will fold itself around every contour of our culture and weigh on every turn of our day. It will cling to all of us who are alive today as well as to our children and grandchildren and even, perhaps, to our great grandchildren, as well.

And yet, when compared to its predecessor, this disruptive interval will happen in a blink of history's eye. The First Middle Ages lasted for almost one thousand years, from the 5th to the 15th century.

Shaped by agriculture and rigid social structures, the sweep of its defining characteristics unfolded slowly as did the changes they imposed on life.[38] The Second Middle Ages will last approximately 100 years, from 2018 to circa 2118. It will be driven by dizzying technological innovation that outstrips the ability of governmental, societal, educational and other institutions to keep up. As a consequence, while the debilitating effects of the First Middle Ages lasted much longer, the concentration of those effects in the Second Middle Ages will magnify the hardships and anguish they impose on America's citizens.

AN ARCHITECTURE OF INCREASING DISRUPTION

Despite the very different lengths of their duration, both the First and Second Middle Ages will unfold in a similar pattern. The First Middle Ages is generally considered to have occurred in three overlapping phases:

- **The Early MA1**, from the 5th to the 11th centuries, was characterized by invasions and mass migrations across Europe, North Africa and the Middle East.

- **The High MA1**, from the 11th to 14th centuries, was characterized by agricultural innovations, population growth and the strife of the Crusades.

- **The Late MA1**, from the 14th to the early 15th century, was characterized by famine, religious and civil unrest and the ruin of the Black Plague.[39]

Similarly, the Second Middle Ages will occur in three overlapping but much shorter phases:

- **The Early MA2**, from 2018 to circa 2040, during which people will move from one career field and industry to another as super-C machines eliminate more and more human jobs in the workplace.

- **The High MA2**, from circa 2040 to circa 2100, during which smart machines will add dizzying new capabilities that will improve corporate productivity and financial performance, even as workers strain to find sufficient employment to provide the basic necessities for themselves and their families.

- **The Late MA2**, from circa 2100 to circa 2118, during which near universal unemployment and the resulting financial crisis will plunge the country into mass deprivation, social turmoil and political dissension, leaving it depleted and in need of a new direction.

All of today's American generations will have to rise to the challenge posed by this trying period. Baby Boomers, Gen-Xers and Millennials will have to overcome the riptides of the Early Second Middle Ages. Gen-Xers, Millennials and Gen-Zs will have to face down the unrelenting tests of the High Second Middle Ages. And, Gen-Zs and their children – Gen-Z Alphas – will have to find the nation's way out of the gloom of the Late Second Middle Ages. Each will establish its own particular legacy, but all will have to be greater than the generation before. Each will have to measure up to the challenges of its time and place in the age, but all must set the foundation for the greatness of the generations that follow.

That heroic tradition makes this period deserving of the adjective Middle. While it is certainly true that the Second Middle Ages will be a discontinuity – a break with our culture's current hyper allegiance to rationalism, empiricism and data – it will also be an interval in America's historic pursuit of a more perfect union. It will stand between the nation's founding commitment to the dignity and goodness of humankind and its ultimate expression in the Age of Ennoblement.

As every grade school child learns, the U.S. Declaration of Independence begins with this powerful, yet simple articulation of the nation's credo:

> "We hold these truths to be self-evident, that all men are created equal, that they are endowed by their Creator with certain unalienable Rights, that among these are Life, Liberty and the pursuit of Happiness."

Despite the profound clarity of those words, the

nation's people have debated, legislated and fought over their essence throughout its two-plus centuries of existence. What does it mean to declare that "all men are created equal? Or, that they "are endowed by their Creator with certain unalienable Rights?" And, what is the definition of those enumerated Rights of "Life, Liberty and the pursuit of Happiness?" The search for those answers – to perfect a union of people – is the great national journey of the United States of America. And technology will, for a time, interrupt it in the Second Middle Ages.

Over the next one hundred years, ever more powerful, ever smarter and intuitive technology will attack the primacy of humankind. It will debase the fundamental value of all people and interfere with their unalienable Rights. It will diminish the quality of their Life, threaten their Liberty, and put their pursuit Happiness in jeopardy. It will not do so, however, as portrayed by Hollywood and a long line of science fiction novelists. Technology will not subvert and ultimately destroy us because it is inherently evil or anti-human. It does not have our worst interests in its circuits and software. Quite the contrary. Technology will disrupt and damage our lives because the mechanisms we humans use to develop it and unleash its power will be blind to the consequences of doing so.

The challenge facing America's four extant generations isn't super-C machines – they can and likely will be a resource for humankind's good. It is, instead, the imperfect process we employ to create those machines. It is the Wild West approach – this land rush on steroids – that has evolved to invent new uses for artificial intelligence, natural language processing, deep learning and neural networks and to capitalize on those inventions in the marketplace before we have figured out the unintended consequences they might also perpetrate. It is the obsessive drive to be the first with each additional level of machine capability and to make a profit or gain fame or both from that position before we understand and manage whatever harm they might inadvertently inflict. That destructive impulse has now intruded itself into America's determined quest to perfect its union, and it will take us one hundred years of hardship to overcome it.

Chapter 6

The Early MA2 – Sporadic Disruption

2018 to Circa 2040

"The time is out of joint. O cursed spite that ever I was born to set it right!"

William Shakespeare, *Hamlet*

The first phase of the Second Middle Ages will begin almost imperceptibly. Initially, it will continue trends already underway prior to 2018, including the occasional public expression of alarm at the potential impact of machine technology on the number of permanent, full-time jobs that are accessible by most American workers and the resulting diminution of their standard of living and quality of life. These warnings will be countered by an almost equal measure of commentary that either denigrates them as nothing more than careless fearmongering or characterizes them as "fake science" similar to the make-believe accounts, they will charge, of those who claim Americans landed on the moon in 1969.

This debate during the early years will unfold in two media channels. The arguments among concerned and unconcerned data scientists, engineers, super-C machine developers and other technology experts will largely play out in research journals and other similarly esoteric publications and therefore be all but invisible to the general public. The exchanges among corporate leaders, HR and workforce experts and social scientists will mostly take place in more accessible professional and business publications, so they will be seen by more of the population, but also do little to arouse widespread concern. They will be read and almost immediately dismissed or forgotten. Even the articles and posts that identify the specific job or occupational categories that are most at risk will generate little concern among either workers at large or those in the crosshairs.

It won't be until sometime in the middle of the phase that a handful of well-known and highly regarded public figures are able to break through the indifference and make the threat real to the public at large. They will finally get working Americans to recognize the disruption super-C machines are having in the workplace and the implications of that creeping domination for their own careers and lives. These thought leaders will have the advantage of several decades worth of workplace data to reinforce their positions, but their success will also be due, in no small measure, to the words and actions of an earlier generation of caution-sayers.

They will continue and extend the warnings of such notable figures as the late Stephen Hawking, the English theoretical physicist and cosmologist; Bill Gates, the Microsoft founder and global philanthropist; and Elon Musk, the CEO of Tesla and SpaceX. Expressed years before the arrival of super-C machines, their concerns were almost always nonspecific and more about policy and process than the technology's impact on specific groups of people or even people in general. They didn't predict the elimination of a particular career field or job category, and they didn't foretell the demise of this or that industry. In effect, they didn't connect the dots to something tangible in the lives of working men and women, but what they did do was almost as important. They established the appropriateness and credibility of raising an alarm about the potential dislocation that could be caused by artificial intelligence.

Musk, for example, was quoted in 2015 as saying that AI researchers could "produce something evil by accident—including, possibly, a fleet of artificial intelligence-enhanced robots capable of destroying mankind."[40] To his credit, he also put his money where his uneasiness was by establishing an organization known as OpenAI. The organization described itself as "a non-profit AI research company, discovering and enacting the path to safe artificial general intelligence."[41] In other words, it would work to develop a way of introducing the technology that could secure its benefits for humankind without diminishing or degrading the very people it was designed to help.

This pre-MA2 era also saw the establishment of a number of watchdog organizations. Driven by their alarm at the unconstrained, head-long rush into the technology's development, they were set up to monitor AI research in the U.S. as well as globally and to establish protocols that would ensure its continued advancement without the specter of unintended and potentially destructive consequences.

AI Austin, for example, was formed with the mission of:

> "encouraging practical and responsible design, development and use of Artificial Intelligence to expand the opportunities and minimize the harm in both local and global communities."[42]

One of its co-founders, Michael E. Stewart, went on to help establish AI Global with a similar mission.

Launched during the same period, the Allen Institute for Brain Science, the creation of Microsoft co-founder Paul Allen, had a somewhat different purpose, but a similar perspective on AI research.

As its Chief Scientific Officer, Christof Koch, put it:

> "Runaway machine intelligence is something we need to think about more …. Clearly, we can't say let's not develop any more AI. That's never going to happen. But we need to figure out what are the imagined dangers and what are the real ones and how to minimize them."[43]

These and other warnings that were issued even before the arrival of the Second Middle Ages failed to move the needle on public consciousness for several reasons. For some in the population, the notion of a machine-dominated world of work was simply too much like the fictions of Hollywood to be credible and thus wasn't anything to worry about. For others, the idea of ultra-smart, ultra-intuitive, ultra-empathetic technology was nothing more than speculation as there were no hard data to confirm what it could – or could not – do in the real world. And for still others immersed in the cynical and argumentative culture of those years, it simply felt better to describe the warnings about super-C machines as nothing more than Chicken Little hollering at the sky.

The first phase of the Second Middle Ages will begin almost imperceptibly.

THE FIRST STIRRINGS
OF CONCERN

Despite the initial misgivings about the situation, peoples' outlook will begin to change before the third decade of the century comes to a close. Even then, it will still be unknowable if humans could and would create Terminator-like machines capable of attacking humankind. What won't be in question as the evidence piles up will be the damage that ever more powerful and smart machines are inflicting on working men and women. The former is the product of humankind's imagination; the latter will be the reality humankind's intelligence has created. As that becomes more and more apparent, as the general discussion of disruption morphs into a specific crisis in individual lives, what was once ignored or maligned will become omnipresent and menacing.

Vast swathes of the American workforce – white collar as well as blue collar workers, executives as well as seasoned professionals and manual laborers, Boomers and Gen-Xers as well as Millennials and Gen-Zs – will be forced into chronic unemployment. Super-C machines won't throw thousands of people out of work. They will throw millions. They won't affect this narrow occupation or that tiny sliver of the job market. They will destroy entire career fields and eliminate jobs in every single industry in the economy.

Even the workers who develop the technology that powers super-C machines will be at risk. Among the advances that will, ironically, evolve from their own work is something called AutoML. It refers to machines that can learn how to build other machines that use machine learning to accomplish a specific task – no human required. Google, for example, has "used the AutoML tech to design networks for image and speech recognition tasks. In the former, the system matched Google's experts. In the latter, it exceeded them, designing better architectures than the humans were able to create."[44] And, it did so prior to 2018. In subsequent years, as that capability matures and is more readily adopted, it will lead to an unprecedented development: the technology will make even technologists irrelevant.

What won't be in question as the years pile up will be the damage that ever more powerful and smart machines are inflicting on working men and women.

The hashtag *#WhatIsHappeningtoUs* will start to trend on social media, and the panic will metastasize. All of a sudden, forgotten or ignored research reports will get rediscovered and shared millions of times. One of the most widely read will be a 2014 study by the Pew Research Center on Information & Technology. Its researchers surveyed leading U.S. scientists, technologists and scholars and found a consensus both on the impact of super-C machines in the world of work and on the timing of that impact. It would occur, they agreed, during the Early Second Middle Ages:

> "The vast majority of respondents to the 2014 Future of the Internet canvassing anticipate that robotics and artificial intelligence will permeate wide segments of daily life by 2025, with huge implications for a range of industries such as health care, transport and logistics, customer service, and home maintenance."[45]

Despite that agreement, however, the same survey respondents had differing views on what those implications would mean for human workers. The survey report noted:

> "But even as they are largely consistent in their predictions for the evolution of technology itself, they are deeply divided on how advances in AI and robotics will impact the economic and employment picture over the next decade."[46]

The World Economic Forum, in contrast, was much more certain about the impact and even more aggressive about the timeline. It predicted there will be a global net loss of 5.1 million jobs within the next two years – by 2020. Their disappearance will force working men and women into unemployment in fields as disparate as:

- office and administrative roles,

- manufacturing and production,

- the arts and entertainment,

- construction and extraction, and

- installation and maintenance.[47]

The consulting firms CBRE and Genesis were even more pessimistic. They predicted that 50 percent of today's occupations will be lost to super-C machines and other AI-based technology by 2025.[48] In non-technical, non-economic, non-policy terms — in basic, everyday parlance — that forecast is the death knell of employment for a huge swath of the American workforce, and that sentence will be imposed within the first ten years of the Early Second Middle Ages. They will not only lose the job they have, they will lose any prospect of finding another.

A GATHERING STORM

Though well-intentioned, legislation passed by the federal government will exacerbate the distress among Americans. By the end of the first decade of MA2, the Tax Cuts and Jobs Act of 2017 will be generally described as the Job Cuts and Unemployment Tax or just J-CUT. One tabloid in New York City will introduce an article on it with the headline, *The Unkindest J-Cut of All*. While the bill was largely sold as a stimulus to job creation – the premise being that lowering the corporate tax rate would lead to more hiring – exactly the opposite will actually occur.

In January of 2018, *The New York Times* described the passage of the legislation this way:

> "A wave of optimism has swept over American business leaders, and it is beginning to translate into the sort of investment in new plants, equipment and factory upgrades that bolsters economic growth, spurs job creation – and may finally raise wages significantly.[49]

While the article focused on the impact of loosening regulations, its words – *investment in new plants, equipment and factory upgrades ... raise wages significantly* – inadvertently described the perfect storm for American's workers.

There were already 6,000,000 open jobs in the U.S. – a record – when the bill was passed in 2017. At the same time, there were 6.8 million Americans looking for work.[50] Employers couldn't fill their openings with those candidates because most were unqualified or unavailable to do the work. Job seekers either didn't have the requisite skills – most notably those requiring a foundation in STEM

– or weren't living where the jobs were located.

As the months go by, that workforce deficit will grow worse – much worse. Indeed, by mid-2018, there were more open positions than there were job seekers looking for employment. Rather than create even more jobs they would struggle to fill, therefore, employers will take the financial windfall created by the tax bill and invest in the development of capital equipment – super-C machines. In effect, they will create more jobs, but those jobs will be filled by byte-collar workers. Even worse, employers will also avoid the potential of escalating wages by deploying machines into many of the jobs still filled by humans, forcing even more people into alternative forms of employment

For many, the sudden loss of their own permanent, full time position coupled with the loss of others for which they could apply will mean a radical shift in their approach to employment. They will have no choice but to become a part-time or temporary worker. According to the U.S. Bureau of Labor Statistics, almost 3.1 million U.S. workers were employed in temporary positions in September of 2017. That amounts to 2.08 percent of the entire American workforce, the highest percentage since the government began keeping records.[51] By 2040, however, that number will triple to 10 million workers – a population almost five times the size of the U.S. military in 2017 and over half the size of total union membership that year.[52, 53]

There will also be similar growth in what's called

the gig workforce. While the line that separates it from the temp workforce is not always clear, there is no doubt that it too will see an influx of workers who can no longer find full time, permanent employment. In 2017, the gig population totaled somewhere between 27 and 35 percent of the American workforce, depending on how the category was defined.[54] Moreover, many of those workers actually chose to gig because doing so gave them more flexibility, personal control or choice in the kind of work they performed.[55] By the end of the first phase of MA2, more than half of all Americans will be gigging, and they will be doing so because they have no other way to support their families.

All of this disruption during the Early Second Middle Ages will be propelled by two dynamics:

DYNAMIC #1: THE STEADILY CREEPING, ALMOST INVISIBLE ASSIMILATION OF AUTOMATION, ARTIFICIAL INTELLIGENCE AND MACHINE LEARNING IN THE WORKPLACE.

Initially, smart technology will be packaged and sold as helpful, even cute "assistants," designed to make work easier or more pleasant for human workers. The first generation will be offered as chatbots – a technology that can, for example, help sales associates with customer service in online retail stores and help recruiters with the avalanche of applicants on employers' career sites. These products will be incredibly useful, freeing their human coworkers from "grunt work" and enabling them to do what they do best – in the case of salespeople, closing the deal with buyers, and in the case of recruiters, engaging with and evaluating candidates. Their capabilities, however, will fall well short of super-C machines, so a second generation of the technology will inevitably appear.

These 2.0 machines will be positioned as "junior partners" to their human colleagues. While human workers will recognize the threat such systems pose to their own jobs, they will console themselves with the knowledge that they are still in charge of the partnership. They will increasingly rely on their byte-collar partners to get their own job done, but they will be the ones making the decisions.

Employers, on the other hand, will see this pairing of humans and smart technology as a proven and entirely appropriate next step in the harnessing of productivity-enhancing machines. In fact, the proof of concept – and thus the rationale for making such an investment – had already been successfully concluded prior to 2018. Demonstrating an astonishingly broad range of functional capabilities, machine partners had been effectively deployed with human workers in such diverse roles as financial advisors, insurance agents and even physicians.

This human-centric partnership will remain in place until the second decade of the phase. Then, the relationship will take an ominous turn. In job-after-job, machines will take the lead and humans will be repositioned as the junior partner. Machines will collect and interpret data, identify and analyze various responses and decide which action to take – all with little input from and no control by their human coworkers. In effect, the "job" of working men and women will be exactly like that performed by monitors in today's driverless cars. They will be nothing more than the backup, failsafe system. And even in that role, their performance will unfortunately be imperfect, and they will, as a consequence, quickly be replaced by a more attentive and capable backup machine.

To acknowledge the subordination of humans in the workplace, a new term will be coined. Those affected will come to be known as **fringe workers**. They will operate at the outer edges of activity, performing tasks that are incidental and increasingly unimportant to an organization's mission or its success. Moreover, their movement to the fringe will fundamentally reshape entire professions and trades. It will begin in finance and accounting, sales and marketing, and IT and then move into engineering, communications and human resources. A columnist for *The New York Times* will describe it as "a tsunami of irrelevancy" sweeping humans out of the workplace.

DYNAMIC #2: A MISSED OPPORTUNITY TO EDUCATE AND PREPARE WORKERS FOR THE DISRUPTION THAT WILL OCCUR DURING THE PHASE.

Sadly, it often takes a disaster of historic proportions to get humans to prepare properly for the all too certain occurrence of calamitous events. For example, shore communities in New Jersey had seen more than a few hurricanes over the years, but it wasn't until they experienced the devastation of Super Storm Sandy that they finally began to reconfigure their beaches, boardwalks and oceanfront homes for today's reality of more potent and frequent storms.

Unfortunately, the same propensity to wait until after the damage has occurred will afflict the workforce in the Early Second Middle Ages. Workers in one community or another will be battered by the rise of super-C machines, but those in adjacent communities will go on with their lives as if nothing has happened. They will feel the pain of their fellow citizens – they will display the native generosity of Americans by donating food and clothing and even money to help out – but they will do nothing to prepare themselves for a similar disaster.

To acknowledge the subordination of humans in the workplace, a new term will be coined. Those affected will come to be known as fringe workers.

Tragically, many of the country's most important institutions will exacerbate this myopia. The federal government will not see the need to monitor the impact of AI technology on the workforce

– failing even to do something as simple as keeping track of how many human workers have been displaced by machines each year. Colleges and universities will continue to enroll and then graduate students with degrees that qualify them for jobs long since rendered obsolete or pushed to the fringe by machines. And, legions of publicly traded as well as privately owned businesses will continue to promote themselves as employee-friendly organizations by solemnly declaring that "people are our most important asset," while replacing them with machines by the tens of thousands.

Even as the phase unfolds and the disruption becomes more visible and pronounced, these institutions will resist the idea that a new reality has overtaken human employment. Their refusal to see the evidence – like the obstinance of the geocentrists who insisted the Earth was the center of the universe – will extend the misperceptions of the people they serve and set them up for greater hardship in the next phase of the Second Middle Ages. Some will simply not be convinced; they will draw a more benign conclusion from the data. Others, however, will recognize the danger, but refuse to speak out because doing so would undermine their own position. They will subordinate the wellbeing of citizens or students or employees to the preservation of a worldview with which they are comfortable and through which they are handsomely rewarded.

As a consequence, Americans will be more aware of what's happening around them than they were at the outset of the Second Middle Ages. They may even understand it better as the data pile up, but emotionally, they will still be unable to accept it. A survey taken near the midpoint of the phase in 2030 will yield the exact same findings as a survey taken 15 years earlier. That 2015 Pew Research Center survey found that almost two-thirds of U.S. workers (65 percent) thought that, within the next 50 years, super-C machines would do most of the work then done by humans. And yet, despite that certainty, four-out-of-five of those workers (80 percent) said they didn't think it would happen to them – their job, at least, would be safe and remain largely unaffected.[56]

A TALE OF TWO ECONOMIES

Institutional ignorance and self-interest will not be the only causes of workers' misperception of the super-C machine threat. The American economy will also play a significant role. Indeed, it will be a mind-wrenching paradox that even as America's workers struggle to keep a foothold in the new workplace of the Early Second Middle Ages – even as they find themselves giving up ever more ground to byte-collar workers – they will live in and benefit from the fruits of the most expansive and prosperous society on Earth.

Super-C machines will power organizations in both the private and public sectors to significantly higher levels of performance. Those who have pension plans invested in the stock market will see the financial stability of those plans improve, while those who own 401(k) portfolios will enjoy significant growth in the value of their investments. Similarly, those who rely on governmental services – be it welfare or social security payments, medical care in VA hospitals or the issuance of a passport by the State Department – will be accommodated without delay and assisted efficiently and effectively. And perhaps most important of all in a consumer-based economy, Americans will be able to buy products far easier than ever before – both offline and on – and trade up to new and more engaging or useful versions of those products the nanosecond they hit the market. Standing on line in front of a tech company store will be as quaint as driving your own car.

Even on-the-job, byte-collar workers will improve the lot of those few human workers who are still employed, regardless of whether they're working in a full time, part time, temporary, gig or fringe capacity. Machines will shoulder the most dangerous and physically demanding jobs, from logging and commercial fishing to construction and long haul trucking. They will fill in for humans when they're sick or on vacation, eliminating forever the overloaded colleague who's forced to pick up the slack. They will do unpleasant and tedious work and stay at it without complaint or even a coffee break, twenty-four hours a day, seven days a week. And, they won't backbite, gossip or post ugly messages about a coworker on social media, which sadly, won't change the behavior of the humans in the workplace but will at least decrease the incidence of such acts.

In effect, America will be two economies – one that diminishes the role of humans and champions the rigor and robustness of machines and another that leverages the rigor and robustness of machines to augment humans' quality of life. As the first phase of the Second Middle Ages draws to a close, those two economies will generally be in balance. Hardships will be real and increasingly widespread, but so too will the benefits of a machine-based economy. And then, the technological singularity will occur, and everything will change.

Chapter 7

The High MA2 – Widespread Disruption

Circa 2040 to Circa 2100

"The First Amendment was designed to allow for disruption of business as usual. It is not a quiet or subdued amendment or right."

Naomi Wolfe

The technological singularity – that point in the development of artificial intelligence when machines become smarter than people – will dramatically accelerate the introduction of super-C machines in all facets of the American economy. The quaint idea of designing machines to outplay humans at chess or Go will be overtaken by the frenzied acquisition of machines that can help businesses beat their competitors in the global marketplace. Enterprise automation kits will become the next big thing as companies of all sizes race to leverage the capabilities of machines that can understand human language and perform whatever task humans assign.

Ironically, the unerring quality of their work will also generate an intolerance for anything less than the same level of perfection from human workers. A book entitled *In Need of Excellence* will hit the bestseller list as companies search for ways to minimize human imperfections. The first firing of a human CEO by a super-C Board of Directors will occur. And, the ZT-2B or Zero Tolerance for Bad Behavior law will be passed, enabling companies to separate for cause any employee found deficient at work in two consecutive performance reviews conducted by machines.

WE ARE MACHINES: HEAR US ROAR

The machine-based economy will be described as the **Mach 10 Expansion**, a paean both to old fashioned measures of speed and to the newly found power of machines. The automated enterprise will be extolled in the textbooks and classrooms of business schools, and most of those institutions will replace their Human Resource specialization with a track that focuses on Machine Resources. Super-C machines will be given human first names and corporate last names and appear as frequently as their human counterparts on the covers of leading business magazines. The dot.com bubble of the late 20th century will be forgotten as private equity firms and venture capitalists firehose money into hundreds of startups, all vying to be the first no-employee Unicorn. It will happen in 2092 when "the only totally autonomous super-C enterprise" will be introduced to public stock markets. Its IPO will set a global record in its first day of trading on the New York Stock Exchange.

Machines will also acquire creative capabilities and even some sentient functionality. They will learn how to write novels and research historical treatises and to compose musical scores and perform in concert series. An Autonomous Best Seller list will be created as a companion to the traditional Fiction and Nonfiction lists, so book readers can find the latest titles by their favorite machine. And the first Machine Entertainment Awards will be presented by the Machine Entertainment Association (MEA), taking their place alongside the Country Music Association, Grammy, Black Entertainment Television and People's Choice Awards.

MacFlicks, an automated enterprise that streams live TV shows into American living rooms and dens, will introduce a series called Dewey. It will become a national obsession as it follows the "birth," learning and eventual employment of a humanoid which viewers will be able to tailor to their own ethnicity and gender. Each week, men, women and children all over the country will stop whatever they're doing and watch as the show chronicles Dewey's "life" in Landhaven, a pretty little mountain resort in North Carolina. The show will gross tens of millions of dollars in advertising fees as it follows Dewey from its first autonomous acts through its advancing intelligence and into its mature phase when it's employed in a local bakery to create custom birthday cakes on demand at any time of the day or night. The store's slogan – We bake Happiness into your life – will become a popular meme throughout the business sector.

The machine-based economy will be described as the Mach 10 Expansion, a paean both to old fashioned measures of speed and the newly found power of machines.

Super-C machines will also find solutions to some of humankind's most vexing problems and failings:

- They will find a cure for the common cold and for most types of cancer, but will still be stumped on the development of a birth control pill for men;

- They will eradicate mosquitos and cockroaches

from the planet, although children will still be able to visit virtual zoos to see insectoids or android versions of these pests;

- They will provide instantaneous fact checking of all statements made in public discourse on the Web, but having learned how to communicate from humans, they will also become master purveyors of online snark;

- They will find a way to efficiently capture and use the energy contained in the sun's rays, transforming utilities into safe, clean operations, although the executives of one Midwest utility will go to jail for dumping leftover oil in a local river;

- They will develop a fool-proof way to detect the use of performance enhancing drugs by Olympic athletes, but the Russian Federation will once again be caught trying to cheat, this time by adding a humanoid to its track and field team at the 2072 Summer Olympics;

- They will discover a drug that eliminates pattern baldness among men by super-invigorating their youthful hair, igniting a boom in sales of hair coloring products and driverless convertibles among men of a certain age; and

- They will devise painless, real time plastic surgery techniques, enabling men and women to reshape their faces and bodies on a daily basis and without unpleasant side effects, which will then create a whole new kind of identity theft problem.

THE HUMAN PREDICAMENT

As beneficial as these and other developments will be, American working men and women will feel battered and forgotten by what is simultaneously happening to them in the workplace. Even as super-C machines advance science and health, the environment and sports, they will move into and take over what few jobs humans still hold during this period. Unemployment will surge as more and more workers are unable to keep pace with the accelerating capabilities of their machine competitors in the job market. Some will simply be unable to do what super-C machines can do, while others will see their skills and knowledge fall further and further behind as machines up the requirements for any human who wants to work with them.

Fifty years after the U.S. enters the Second Middle Ages, the tradition of steady, full time employment in America – the institution that was the foundation for the country's reputation as a "land of opportunity" – will succumb to a new **Artificial Manifest Destiny**. It will articulate the view that the expansion of super-C machines into the full reaches of America's workplace is both advantageous to and appropriate for the nation. Though controversial and, in some quarters at least, rejected as "algorithmic jingoism," it will eventually take on an aura of historical inevitability and become the country's guiding doctrine.

Shortly thereafter, human work opportunities will become entirely transient. The U.S. staffing industry – estimated to be a $146.6 billion market in 2018[57] – will triple by 2070, and force two dramatic changes in the country. First, Americans will return to living together in extended families so they have more minds and bodies to chase the dwindling supply of employment opportunities. And second, the members of each family will piece together a mélange of part-time, temporary and gig work just to keep a roof over their heads and meals on the table.

The hunting and gathering for food by ancient tribes will be updated with the searching and applying for jobs by modern ones. And even that survival strategy will be at risk. The sick employees, sudden spike in new orders and ad hoc crises that often create the need for temps and part-timers will no longer have that effect. Machines will not need to take mental health days and be immune to the Day After Super Bowl Flu. They can and will be supplemented with additional Capacity as a Cloud (CaaC) technologies or simply be reconfigured to work additional hours or days whenever the need arises.

THE TURNING POINT

The despair felt by the ever-growing numbers of

unemployed and underemployed workers will be heightened and turned to anger as the gulf between them and the country's economic elites widens and grows more visible. The point-one percenters – especially a certain cohort of those who "earn" their living in investment banks, hedge funds and other financial enterprises – will be unaffected by the disruption in the workplace for one simple reason: their income isn't derived from employment, but from property or capital. These 21st century feudal barons, like their predecessors in the First Middle Ages, will see themselves as superior to everyone else in the country (by virtue of their genius, wealth, physical appearance or family name) and be indifferent to the hardships they are enduring.

As Rana Foroohar pointed out in her 2016 book, *Makers & Takers: The Rise of Finance and the Fall of American Business*, "... the financial sector now represents around 7% of the U.S. economy, up from 4% in 1980. Despite taking around 25% of all corporate profits, it creates a mere 4% of all jobs."[58] She went on to argue that this investment of capital in capital rather than in new businesses – traditionally one of the main engines of American economic growth – has further depressed the creation of new jobs.[59] Therefore, not only will these financial princes and princesses continue to build their pseudo-empires of wealth, the way they do so will further undermine the employment prospects of workers. They will live in luxury while the rest of the population will struggle just to get by. They will be indifferent to the plight of others even as the ranks of the impoverished grow around them. One scion of an uber-wealthy family in Greenwich, Connecticut will be overheard saying, "Let them eat some of Dewey's cake."

Fifty years after the U.S. enters the Second Middle Ages, the tradition of steady, full time employment in America - the institution that was the foundation for the country's reputation as a "land of opportunity" - will succumb to a new Artificial Manifest Destiny.

Town hall meetings held by Congressional Representatives and Senators will erupt in anger as speaker-after-speaker denounces the Government's inability to rectify the situation. Protest marches will draw tens of thousands of people, all demanding that something be done. They will be rallied by a gravelly-voiced singer from Asbury Park, New Jersey, who will pay homage to an earlier son of that city and to those the nation is mistreating with the anthem, *Stillborn in the USA*. Within days, the song's name will be scrawled across store fronts and city park benches, sidewalks and even municipal buildings all across the country.

The anger will grow so widespread that the federal government will finally be roused from its lethargy and take up a number of proposals to address it. A bipartisan group in Congress will introduce a bill for a new tax on the income of the uber-rich and coalesce into a new political party – the Anti-Oligarchs – to push its passage. As with all modern third party attempts, it will fail to unseat many Republicans or Democrats in either the House or the Senate, but it will force both parties to talk about income inequality in the country and to propose measures to address it. Neither, however, will call out the oligarchs themselves as the source of the problem, but will instead point their fingers at the "vicious incursion" of super-C machines. A Congressman with aspirations of higher office, will go so far as to call it an "automated Pearl Harbor."

The deflection will work and Congress's access to wealthy patrons will be preserved. No bills will be introduced, no legislation will be passed, and no action will be taken to limit the access and influence of the oligarchs. Members will privately breathe a sigh of relief and turn their attention to – as a four-term Senator put it – "fixing this robot-run-amuck problem."

Despite this setback, their constituents will keep up the pressure, leading eventually to the formation of a rump caucus of both Representatives and Senators who are determined to find a more impactful solution. Though they share that common goal, however, the group will quickly splinter into several factions, each supporting a different approach to the problem. One camp of politicians will demand that the technology be stuffed back into the genie's bottle. It's simply too dangerous to be adequately controlled, they will argue, analogizing it to virtual uranium. They will gather millions of followers, but also be ridiculed by the technorati on both coasts as LDLs or Latter Day Luddites.

A second camp will take exactly the opposite tact. They will declare that there is "blame on both sides" of the human-machine conflict, essentially establishing the moral equivalence of the two parties. They will go on to argue that the ever-expanding capabilities of machines make them deserving of more standing and respect in a democratic economy. They will even take up a position articulated earlier in the 21st century that robots have rights similar to those of humans, and just as humans cannot have their freedom circumscribed, neither can robots (or other smart machines).[60] Finally, as the century draws to a close in 2099, they will propose the 29th Amendment – called by some the Machine Citizenship Act – which would grant to machines all of the rights specified for humans in all previous Amendments to the Constitution.

The debate over these and all of the other proposals circulating through Congress and society at large will end as this phase of the Second Middle Ages comes to a close. It will conclude not because one side or the other makes their case more persuasively, but because it is overtaken by events. The economic circumstances of a majority of Americans will have grown so dire as to represent an existential threat to the nation.

The record climb of the stock market achieved through the rapid and widespread introduction of super-C machines in the early years of the Second Middle Ages will come to a screeching halt as unemployment surges through every city and town. The declining income of American consumers – that ever-reliable engine of the U.S. economy – will send a shock wave of dramatically lower sales and profits through America's businesses, from its largest enterprises to the mom and pop shops lining Main Street. Hospitals will be inundated with patients who need medical attention or medicine, but cannot pay for either. Banks will see homeowners by the tens of thousands default on their mortgages. And cities and towns will have so many residents in arrears on their tax payments, they can no longer reliably pick up the trash or keep the streets clean.

The prospect of a socio-economic collapse will finally forge a national consensus that something has be done. Political parties, unions, professional societies and trade associations, even the private sector's powerful army of K Street lobbyists in Washington, D.C. will all agree that action – immediate, comprehensive and impactful enough to redress the situation – must be taken. What they will not agree on is exactly what the country should do.

Weeks, then months will pass with no resolution. Proposals and counter proposals will be floated, debated and eclipsed by still other proposals. Representatives in the House will hold committee meetings and debate for the handful of viewers still watching CSPAN; the Administration will hold Cabinet meetings and provide a phalanx of spokespersons for the Sunday morning talk shows streamed to their viewers' virtual reality window blinds. Newspapers will publish editorials decrying the lack of swift action, and pundits will rush out books calling for this or that solution. Billions of words will be spoken, written, tweeted and retweeted, but no action will result. One wag will suggest that global warming has been accelerated with all the hot air blowing through the nation's capital. The words of the Bard, however, provide the best description – it will be a storm of sound and fury signifying nothing.

Then, in the early days of 2100, a petition submitted by a Community Job Club in Trumbull, Connecticut to WhiteHouse.gov will garner over five million signatures in just twenty-four hours. The government's server will crash and then crash again. When it's finally back online, an additional eight million signatures will be added to the petition in just three days.

This platform for ordinary citizens to make their elected government pay attention to issues of importance to them had originally been launched during the Obama Administration way back in the early days of the 21st century. Subsequent Presidents mothballed the site until 2065, when it will be revived by a President worried about the country's sinking morale. Thirty-five years after that, the first post-Generation Z President, representing a cohort called the Gen-Z-Alphas, will be so struck by the petition that she will make the concerns it raises the centerpiece of her Administration. Within days, her West Wing team will draft a bill to mobilize the nation and confront the peril of machine-induced near universal unemployment.

The legislation will create two new programs even more radical and disruptive to traditional norms than those President Franklin Delano Roosevelt introduced in the Great Depression of the 20th century. His successor more than one hundred and fifty years later will face an equally monumental challenge, but she will see a very different role for her bill. Instead of pulling the country out of a terrible downturn in the economy, she will envision lifting the country above such cycles. For that reason, she will call her initiative the Great Aspiration Act of 2100.

Unlike the macro-economic solutions of the past, this legislation will lay the groundwork for a societal restructuring that brings the country back to its first principles of liberty and justice for all. To achieve that goal, the bill will establish a set of new taxes that will fully subsidize both healthcare insurance and a basic income for all Americans. It will also declare working men and women free of involuntary employment for others and establish their right to pursue work that enables them to achieve both self-actualization and self-transcendence.

The bill will be a truly revolutionary initiative and, not surprisingly, within minutes of its introduction in the Congress, it will be hit with a fierce counter-assault. The leaders of this contra movement will highlight the costs and turmoil associated with transforming the nation from an employment-centric economy to what they will label "America's handout society." They will denounce what they see as the bill's dissolution of the country's historic achievement-based class structure and its replacement with a "participant trophy culture" that opens the door to an unknown but indisputably less than meritocratic future.

The opposition will burn bright for several weeks. A Senator from Texas will hold a press conference where he will unveil a ten foot tall trophy emblazoned with *Presented to the Freeloader-in-Chief.* He'll rail against the bill, all the while referring to the President as Madam Moocher, but be heckled so loudly by the crowd that he'll stop halfway through his prepared remarks and ride off in a limousine provided by a sympathetic lobbyist.

After that, resistance will fade and with letters and email running 1,000 to 1 in favor of The Great Aspiration Act, the bill will be passed into law as the High Second Middle Ages draws to a close circa 2100. America will have become a full-fledged Tier Two Society. The physical and security needs of its citizens will have been met. But beyond that certainty, there will still be a mystery that remains unresolved. There will still be a question the country hasn't answered. What will Americans do with this 2.0 version of their independence?

Chapter 8

The Late MA2 – Near Total Disruption
Circa 2100 to Circa 2118

"But there was a special kind of gift that came with embracing the chaos, even if I cursed most of the way. I'm convinced that, when everything is wiped clean, it's life's way of forcing you to become acquainted with and aware of who you are now, who you can become. What is the fulfillment of your soul?"

Jennifer DeLucy

At his May, 2017 Harvard University commencement speech, Facebook's chief executive Mark Zuckerberg had some tough words for the graduating class. "Our generation will have to deal with tens of millions of jobs replaced by automation like self-driving cars and trucks," he said, adding, "When our parents graduated, purpose reliably came from your job, your church, your community. But today, technology and automation are eliminating many jobs. Membership in communities is declining. Many people feel disconnected and depressed, and are trying to fill a void."[61]

So, what advice did he offer as a solution? What did he suggest these new graduates do to prepare for the challenges they would face in the years ahead? Not one to think small, he gave them this charge: "Class of 2017, you are graduating into a world that needs purpose. It's up to you to create it." He then went on to say, "Taking on big meaningful projects is the first thing we can do to create a world where everyone has a sense of purpose. The second is redefining equality to give everyone the freedom they need to pursue purpose."[62]

As those in the audience would eventually learn, this notion of pursuing purpose in one's life was hardly a new idea. A browser search of the term *purpose in life* yielded 19,300,000 results in 2017. Among the most famous sources, of course, was Rick Warren's 2007 best seller, *A Purpose Driven Life*. His book was a daily guide to Christian living in the 21st century and sold over 30 million copies.[63] Other sources described very different pathways to living purposefully. These included being useful and making a difference, tapping the fullness of life's experiences, being as much of oneself as possible, and shaping one's life with deeply held values.

This diversity of expression makes clear that the definition of a purposeful life is not universal, but is instead, intensely personal. It is a defining attribute of one's life that each person identifies and pursues for him or herself. A purposeful life is unique to the person who lives it, but always includes not one, but two facets. In every case, purpose only becomes real and achievable if it is associated with both the expression of one's talent in an endeavor they consider meaningful and worthwhile and the search for answers to questions only humans value and can answer. A purposeful life is one that is both savored within the dimensions of physical existence and touched in some way by the infinite beyond it.

Sadly, by the time the Late MA2 arrives, it will be clear that Zuckerberg's exhortation about leading such a life will have had little impact. Many if not most of the graduates he addressed that May day will fail to accomplish the mission he challenged them to accept. They will become successful bankers and surgeons, writers and musicians, business leaders and government officials, but they will not lead a purposeful life. They will be held back by the handcuffs of paid employment and erroneous assumptions about talent and wealth. And, they will be unable to pull themselves out of a cultural miasma in America that for a time feeds humankind's worst impulses and suffocates its best.

Their children and grandchildren, on the other

hand, will not be similarly derailed. They will have the benefit of a societal and economic foundation that enables them to establish a new reality for America. In this 22nd century version of the country, they will achieve purpose. They will make it a part of their lives. And, they will take on big projects to do so. Big projects that reshape the warp and woof of their day and the depth and richness of their wonder at its possibilities.

THE QUEST FOR
SELF-ACTUALIZATION

The new approach to purpose won't be manifest or even widely recognized right away. In fact, quite the opposite will occur. The early years of the Late Second Middle Ages will collapse into a dark hole of every human-hurtful trend found in the Early and High periods. Super-C machines and byte-collar workers will finally take over almost every job in America. Professions, crafts and trades will become obsolete, at least as a means for paid employment. The careers of human workers will collapse, at least as they were understood in the Industrial and Information Ages. Near universal unemployment will occur, at least when employment is defined as working for a paycheck and someone else's benefit. And, a nation built on industry, determination and a can-do spirit, will find itself out of things to do, goals to accomplish and rewards to earn.

Contrary to expectations based in old-fashioned economic thought, however, this new reality will not be the cause of either great suffering or a sense of great loss. By the midpoint of the phase, the Great Aspiration Act will have so transformed American culture that the absence of any requirement to work for someone else will be celebrated and revered. Americans will sense that technology has both disrupted their lives and given them access to a different kind of purpose than their parents or grandparents had or could even imagine.

These 22nd century Americans will have the time, the energy and the financial wherewithal to do work that enables them to apply their capacity for excellence in roles about which they are truly passionate. Their days will no longer be a daily grind of mind-numbing work as a cog in the system of some soulless enterprise. Instead, they will rise each day and be able to do purposeful work: to share their talent with organizations committed to missions they find meaningful and worthwhile.

They will tutor kids in Appalachia and build houses for the homeless in New York City. They will plant trees in fire-scorched areas of California and restock fisheries in Washington. They will staff recovery centers after a tornado in Iowa, and they will help immigrants get settled in North Carolina. A diverse people, Americans will find a myriad of ways to do good work and make a difference ... both for others and for themselves.

They will also exercise that same sense of purpose elsewhere around the world. The Peace Corps will be renamed the Aspiration Corps (or A-Corps for short), and Americans of all ages will flock to its projects. They will dig wells to deliver clean water for villagers in east Africa and administer vaccines to the poor in Bangladesh. They will teach girls as well as boys in Afghan schoolhouses, and they will shore up crumbling roads and bridges in Central America.

Unlike in the 20th and 21st centuries when budgets limited their size and scope, these projects will be expansive enough to touch millions in the U.S. and millions more in other countries. The people who are involved won't actually be employed by the organizations with which they are working, but will instead serve as unpaid volunteers. In effect, they will be self-employed, not to earn a living, but to earn a deep and enduring sense of living purposefully.

For many, it will be the only way they can use the skills and knowledge they acquired for a career – as a doctor or engineer or a teacher or social worker. For others, it will be their only access to a role that no longer exists for humans – as an electrician or teamster or a carpenter or roughneck. And for still others, it will be the joyful response to a calling that, until the end of paid employment, they were unable to experience or even to discover. Regardless of how or why they do it, however, the work will be their pathway to self-actualization. It will give them a consequential aspiration and the dignity that comes from accomplishing it.

After almost one hundred years of hardships and

ego-deflating changes in the workplace, American workers will begin to feel good about themselves once again. They will reassert their native optimism, recover their national swagger and rediscover the Happiness that comes from doing work that actually benefits others by serving their well-being rather than some bottom line. There will still be a cabal of money-grubbers on Wall Street and in hedge funds, but most Americans will leverage their UHI/UBI to perform tasks that apply their capacity for excellence to the betterment of their fellow citizens, their country or their planet.

No less important, their work will reinforce America's reputation for kindness and generosity around the globe. It will retire the 20th and 21st century figure known as the Ugly American and install in its stead a more accurate image for the country's people – the Better American. It will establish (or some would say, refurbish) a national reputation for selfless devotion to the betterment of others. This reacquired societal brand will stand in stark, illuminating contrast to the give-something-to-get-something, self-serving behavior of certain Asian and Middle Eastern countries.

Americans' redefinition of purpose will also change the way the country sees and treats itself. The shift will be subtle at first, but it will eventually lead to a reversal in our society's polarity. We will move from a national obsession with our shortcomings and misdeeds to a celebration of our highlights and good deeds. It won't change our determination to root out the worst about ourselves, but instead balance that commitment with one that nurtures the best of us.

An entrepreneurial student at Tufts University in Boston will start selling T-shirts emblazoned with Make America Celebrate Again, and the hashtag #MACA will trend for awhile on Twitter. The media will recognize the importance (and commercial opportunities) of this shift and follow suit with a new form of journalism called *inspirational reporting*. While investigative reporting will still play a central role in newscasts, this parallel approach will create programming that features the good work people are doing in the country, and that programming will get equal time and promotion on many media outlets.

Not to be outdone, a group of entertainment and sports stars will fund the creation of the Good Works Awards, an annual ceremony to recognize and honor "ordinary" Americans for their contributions to the wellbeing of others. They will also add their celebrity to the event, making its red carpet pre-show and awards presentation ceremony – dubbed the Goodies – the most watched program ever on many media outlets. A 30-second commercial on the televised program for the 2115 event will cost fifteen million dollars, and advertisers will line up to pay the fee.

THE PARALLEL QUEST FOR SELF-TRANSCENDENCE

As the years pass, Americans will both revel in their self-actualization and realize that, no matter how much fulfillment and satisfaction the experience provides, it is not the best they can do. Or be. That view won't be universal, of course, but a majority of the population will come to understand that humans are not only capable of animate excellence, they are endowed with a singular urge to venture beyond themselves and into the metaphysical realm. They can and do aspire to transcendence. They have both the capacity and the drive to seek answers to spiritual questions. Whether it's accomplished through faith in an established religion or their adherence to mysticism or some other form of devotion, whether it happens in private prayer or in group meditation, they seek a connection with what is sacred and profound.

That sense of a second magnetic pole in their lives will fly in the face of the technological foundation on which their lives are based circa 2118. For years, many in the scientific community have argued that as humankind becomes more STEM adept and more empirically grounded, the need for religion would disappear. The drive to explain the unexplainable by ascribing it to some force or power or being over and above humans would become unnecessary as humans ascend in their understanding of the universe. As the late Stephen Hawking put it, "Before we understood science, it was natural to believe that God created the universe, but now science offers a more convincing explanation."[64]

It was a seemingly unassailable worldview as super-C machines began to emerge, but ironically, it would weaken as those machines and the science with which they are built freed up humans to think more deeply about themselves and the world they inhabit. Liberated from their age-old requirements for survival, they could begin to probe the questions only humans can ask and answer — the Why, Where, What and How of their existence. Ironically, technology would turn into the Great Emancipator of human spirituality.

This access to metaphysical exploration will be the other defining dynamic of the Age of Ennoblement. People will join prayer and meditation groups both online and in their neighborhoods; they will take courses in theology and philosophy and attend lectures by spiritual leaders; and they will spend hours analyzing the commentary posted on blogs and downloaded into their implanted neuro-readers. Even old-fashioned books will enjoy a resurgence of support, and *The New York Times* will establish a Spirituality Best Sellers list. But perhaps most surprising, a *#PutThemDown* movement will arise to encourage people to set aside their cell phones and video games so they have some quiet space where they can think about how they would answer those metaphysical questions.

Unfortunately, the past will once again be prologue, and some of this activity will veer off into antisocial or even illegal behavior. One person who describes himself as a "scriptural zealot" will found a cult that abuses children under the guise of "teaching them to behave spiritually." Federal authorities will raid the cult's camp and arrest the adults, but not before they burn its buildings to the ground.

Another person styling herself as the "high priestess of orphans" will hold virtual religious services where she will solicit donations for the care of her flock. Her online tent revivals will attract huge crowds and raise millions of dollars. Within a year, however, she too will be arrested when it's discovered there are no orphans or even any flock. She was using the money to pay for shopping sprees in Europe and vacations at posh resorts in the Caribbean.

As the years pass, Americans will both revel in their self-actualization and realize that, no matter how much fulfillment and satisfaction the experience provides, it is not the best they can do.

These situations will be aberrations, however, and most Americans will go about their spiritual work in a forthright and conscientious manner. That devotion will increasingly be seen as normal or even ordinary behavior, although it will simultaneously raise legal concerns. While such activity will be recognized as constitutionally protected, its sheer magnitude will cause both government officials and many citizens to worry about its potential influence on the nation's culture and affairs. Some will form watchdog groups to ensure the country maintains its historical separation of church and state. Others will lobby on behalf of the "non-spiritual" — atheists and agnostics — and demand that their activities receive equal treatment with those of spiritual groups in public venues and programs. And still others will be organized to monitor both textbooks and classrooms in public elementary and high schools so that no conscious or unconscious proselytizing by teachers or staff creeps in.

Despite these concerns, a majority of Americans will spend a portion of every day engaged in spiritual endeavors. That development will be widely reported by local TV stations and newspapers and almost always include interviews with local citizens. When these individuals are asked what benefit they derive from these practices, most will give not one, but two answers.

First, they will say, it enables them to achieve a deeper and richer appreciation for the human experience. And then, they will add that their spirituality also helps them reassert their superiority over the machines that have taken over so much of their lives. They will explain that their search for answers to humankind's unique questions enables them to reach for self-transcendence – a connection with the sacred or mystical – and, at the same time, to believe once again in humankind's preeminent position on planet Earth. After all, they will conclude, machines can never be taught or learn how to be spiritual or to achieve the tranquility it produces.

THE PERFECTION OF WORK

Entering the Age of Ennoblement will be an arduous, even mind-wrenching experience for many, maybe even most Americans. Reaching for not one but two pinnacles of human endeavor – self-actualization and self-transcendence – will not come naturally to many people. Indeed, it will confront them with challenges so momentous that meeting them will alter the very core of their being. They will be obliged to be more honest, more intrusive and more unblinking in their self-analysis than ever before. And then, they will have to hammer and chisel at their sense of themselves until finally, they have reshaped their self-image and their life's purpose.

In the quest for self-actualization, there are some, of course, who are born knowing what they most enjoy doing at work and what they do best when engaged in that work. They are the lucky exceptions to the general rule, however. Most Americans will have to learn new concepts and unlearn old ones in order to employ themselves at fulfilling jobs. They will have to acquire more knowledge, additional skills, a recast set of priorities, and an alternative way to find purpose in their day.

Most importantly, they will have to believe that no matter their station in society, their income level or degree of experience, their beginnings or even their setbacks, they have been endowed with talent. They will have to acknowledge and discover their own capacity for excellence. And then, they will have to learn how to search for and find their calling – the endeavor which allows them to experience and express that talent in meaningful work. They will have to see themselves as a noble contributor and live in and up to that role.

Similarly, in the quest for self-transcendence, there are some people who find their spiritual pathway early in life. Whether it's the religion of their parents or a faith they discover on their own, they are comfortable with its doctrine, practices and community and devote themselves to them. For everyone else, even the concept of spirituality is a mystery. They will have to be introduced to the possibility of a spiritual aspect in their life and determine if they want to pursue it. And if they choose to do so, they will then have to find the religion or spiritual practice that best suits them.

Regardless of whether or not a person chooses to participate in a religion or spiritual practice, however, they will have to acknowledge the right of all other citizens to do so. They will have to respect every person's right to practice whatever faith they choose and to do so in a society that both reveres its importance and rejects its formal adoption. Their personal decision cannot in any way affect their acceptance of the religious or spiritual behavior of their fellow citizens. They cannot pick and choose what seems reasonable or appropriate to them, but must instead, accept the social legitimacy of every faith and thus the propriety of every individual's manner of worship or rituals. In effect, they must see themselves as a noble person and live in and up to that being.

Together these two endeavors – self actualization and self-transcendence – will fundamentally alter the nature of work. Historically, humans have leased their capabilities, if not their talent, to employers in return for financial compensation. The work they performed produced an output or outcome with a value that accrued almost entirely to their employer. That organization or individual realized the vast majority of the benefit derived from each person's work, whether that benefit was measured in profit, market share or some other metric. From the employer's perspective it was the perfect two-fer – it paid out a wage and got back both work and the measurable benefit that work generated. From the individual's point of view, however, the bargain was a one-sided affair. Yes, their paycheck (hopefully) enabled them to cover their tier two needs, but the value of their work was lost. It provided little or no benefit to them – a vacuum that will finally be filled by the shift to self-ennobling work.

In the new era that emerges circa 2118, employers will rely on byte-collar workers to accomplish most if not all of the work required to produce an output or outcome that generates a beneficial metric. Their value chain will remain intact. Human workers, in contrast, will have their tier two needs met by the UHI/UBI, so they will be able to work at endeavors that generate value for them. They will, for the first time, have the opportunity to realize for themselves their own perfect two-fer

– they will work at their talent and their spirituality and get back the benefits of fulfillment and tranquility. When they do, they will have used work to raise themselves to a higher plane of being. They will have achieved the perfection of work, transforming it into a pathway to their own nobility.

A CENTURY
OF CONTINUOUS
RECALIBRATION

Americans will spend much of the Second Middle Ages trying to understand and then adjust to the new reality it will produce. If those in the workforce during that period – Boomers, Gen-Xers, Millennials, Gen-Zs and Gen-Z-Alphas – are going to be able to move America beyond it, they will have to reset themselves and refocus the nation's institutions. They will have to overcome their fear of machines and their fear of the changes those machines will impose on their lives. They will have to see the end stage of the Industrial and Information Ages not as a catastrophe, but as the beginning stage of a new era that can be far better. And then, they will have to take steps as individuals and as a nation to eliminate or replace outdated roles and rules. They will have to demand change in their government, their education system and their civic and social structures. In short, they will have to treat the Second Middle Ages as a century of continuous recalibration.

Only after that change passage has been completed, only after they have laid the individual and collective foundation for their access to ennoblement through self-actualization and self-transcendence – only after they have adequately readied themselves and the nation – will they be able to take the last and most important step, the one that will launch them into the Age of Ennoblement. That step will both confirm their understanding of their purpose and be the ultimate test of it.

They will explain that their search for answers to humankind's unique questions enables them to reach for self-transcendence - a connection to the sacred or mystical - and, at the same time, to believe once again in humankind's preeminent position on planet Earth.

Their final act of separation from the Second Middle Ages will be to see their ability to reach for nobility as a privilege they alone have been accorded. Of all the species on Earth, only humans have the capacity and the urge to realize their purpose. Other species can love and show kindness. They can be joyful and curious, adaptive and even thoughtful. But, they cannot comprehend or experience the quest for fulfillment and tranquility. That is something only humans can do.

This privilege is humankind's most precious gift, but it is not one that we humans possess. It is an inherent part of our being, but we do not own or control it. And for that reason, we also cannot transfer it to other species or even share it with them. We can't teach it to dolphins or gorillas or embed it in a cell or bacterium. And, as the Late Second Middle Ages unfolds, we will come to understand that the same is true with regard to machines. We cannot code actualization and transcendence into software or the cloud or embed it in networks or algorithms.

Everything else that we associate with being human, we can – and we will – give away to our byte-collar coworkers. We will give them our:

- Ability to speak

- Ability to comprehend human speech

- Ability to interpret human emotions from speech

- Ability to read and understand facial expressions

- Ability to converse with humans, regardless of their language, age or education

- Ability to learn

- Ability to self-teach

as well as our:

- Physical strength

- Physical agility

- Physical endurance

- Knowledge

- Memory

- Intelligence

- Reasoning

- Analysis

- Creativity

- Empathy.

All of that and more is transferable. And every bit of it will be installed in machines. It may be called artificial, but it will be as real as carbon-based life. It may not be human, but it is and will continue to be an undeniable aspect of the human experience.

What is supra-real — what is a higher state of reality — and thus can't be given away is a human's access to nobility. No matter how technologically sophisticated humans may become, no matter how much money they invest in trying to accomplish it, they cannot transfer to or share the quest for purpose in life with the machines they create. It is a gift that humans lack the agency to re-gift even to the most advanced of super-C machines. Those brilliant devices are simply incapable of learning it or even of mimicking it. This higher state – this ripeness of consciousness – is uniquely human, and when we finally accept that, when we emerge from the hardships and limitations of the Second Middle Ages and at last acknowledge and cherish that gift – at that moment circa 2118 – the Neonaissance will begin.

Chapter 9

The Shove Felt Round the Country

"It is in the turmoil of chaos that we discover what, if anything, we are."

Orson Scott Card

What will shove Americans out of the disruption of the Late Second Middle Ages and into the transformative era of the Neonaissance? What will cause the country's men and women, tradespeople and professionals, careerists and 8-to-5ers to accept a whole new purpose in life?

Why would people, who have spent every single day of the Industrial and Information Ages competing with one another to win in the world of business, to establish themselves as successful entrepreneurs, to become masters of the universe or titans of capitalism – why would they suddenly accept the challenge (and the opportunity) of work that focuses, instead on their talent and spirituality?

Why would others who have long defined themselves by their occupational field – they work as doctors or engineers or salespeople or truck drivers or teachers or machinists – why would they abruptly reimagine themselves outside the workplace of paid employment where they have historically derived so much of their identity and sense of self-worth?

Why would a nation that has long revered "the good life" and built its culture and economy on the individual acquisition of as much wealth as possible – whether it's measured in their take-home pay, the size of their home, the stores in which they shop or the cars they drive – why would these champions of dollar-denominated success be willing to re-center their lives on fulfillment and tranquility instead?

TWO SOCIETAL CONCUSSIONS

There are, of course, other ways that people could react to the rise of super-C machines besides a commitment to self-actualization and self-transcendence. They could, for example, pursue a strategy of containment. They could elect a government that promises to impose tough new regulations on employers – an Equal Opportunity/Affirmative Action program for humankind – that requires them to hire a diverse workforce of machines and people. Or, they could outlaw the development of artificial intelligence and machine learning beyond a certain point and threaten those who violate that standard with fines and civil penalties. And, they could also be more confrontational and extreme. They might, for example, organize guerrilla campaigns that send people into offices and factories in the dead of night to sledge hammer the offending machines so employers would have no choice but to hire humans to get the work done.

These and other forms of resistance will almost certainly emerge in America over the next one hundred years. They will be controversial, but also attract considerable support. As much as thirty to thirty-five percent of the population will — with some justification — feel abandoned and left unprotected by the country's political and business leadership. They will seethe with anger and lash out at the institutions that have let them down.

Their fellow citizens, however, will not follow suit. They will see these tactics for what they are: societal dead-ends. They will acknowledge the hardships machines are imposing on American workers, but also rightly describe such moves as 21st century versions of the Luddite revolt and just as doomed to failure.

Unfortunately, this larger group – a majority of Americans – will lack a unifying view that could serve as a plausible alternative to resistence. As a consequence, the country will lurch through a period of confusion and aimlessness. Simply understanding what is happening, let alone adjusting to the new reality it imposes, will seem beyond the reach of individual citizens as well as their civic and social institutions. History will offer no roadmap and precedent will provide no guidelines for devising an appropriate response to the onset of ever-widening unemployment. The situation will be so incomprehensible and so overwhelming, it might as well be an extraterrestrial invasion.

That disorientation will become the new norm in America. It will throw the country's people into a psychological dungeon where they are forced to acknowledge their loss of control over and sense of security in their lives. It will deny them principles on which they have always counted and isolate them from truths in which they have always believed. Worst of all, it will starve their native loyalty — their innate allegiance to their country — and torture them with a wrenching migraine of loss as their banishment from the workplace becomes real and irreversible.

They will remain locked up in this confusion until early in the 22nd century, when they finally begin to feel the need for release. At first, it will be nothing more than an undertone of impatience with their condition when they are alone with their thoughts. The disquietude will feed on itself, however, and before long it will present as a nagging conviction that they can and must be better, even as they remain locked in paralysis. They will, at one and the same time, be certain of what needs to be done and unable to stir themselves to action. They will chafe at their passivity, yet be too intimidated to take the first step. They will know they must act, but still hold back from the search for an alternative – a response that would provide both a credible way forward and a genuine reason for hope.

This situation will have the potential to push the country into an irreversible social psychosis. It will be powerful enough to dim the vision and sap the energy of its people forever. It happened to Babylon and the Minoans of Crete, to the totem builders on Easter Island and to the Maya and the Nabateans, so it could decimate the United States of America, as well. This sickness of human consciousness and confidence could rob the country of its future. But, it won't.

The American people will escape a societal collapse, although it will not be with a collective sigh of relief. They will be directed to an alternative course for the nation – one that will take them into the Age of Ennoblement – not by logic or reason or great leadership, but by two concussive factors – two blows to their national psyche. One is already destabilizing the nation and clouding peoples' vision of its future. The other will do so within the next two decades. Together, they will force Americans to see the parallel expressions of individual talent and spirituality as the only viable way out of the Second Middle Ages.

These two societal concussions are:

- **The Melancholic Plague.** Just as the infectious Black Plague inflicted widespread suffering and disillusionment during the First Middle Ages, a plague of dispiriting behavior among the country's business, political and cultural elites and a segment of its general public will rock the morale and self-confidence of Americans in the Second Middle Ages and push them to seek relief in the Neonaissance.

- **The Technological Singularity.** The relentless incursion of ultra-smart, hyper-intuitive and increasingly empathetic technology – super-C machines – into every aspect of the economy during the Second Middle Ages will sever American's access to paid employment and push them to work, instead, on reaching for the nobility only humans can achieve and only the Neonaissance will recognize and celebrate.

The Melancholy Plague will have already begun to undercut the health of American society even before the Second Middle Ages begins. It will fester and worsen throughout the Early and High Middle Ages. The Technological Singularity, in contrast, won't occur until the High Second Middle Ages, and its full effects won't be felt for more than fifty years. It will begin to reshape the American workplace just as the Melancholy Plague reaches its high point in the Late Second Middle Ages, and their simultaneous impact will shove the United States into the Neonaissance.

THE MELANCHOLIC PLAGUE

The infectious Black Plague decimated social structures; religious, academic, governmental and commercial institutions; and the lives of millions of individuals in Europe, the Middle East and Asia. The pandemic was a complex of three diseases, each of which took a terrible toll:

- The bubonic plague, with a mortality rate of 30 to 75 percent of an infected population;

- The pneumonic plague, with a mortality rate of 90 to 95 percent of an infected population; and

- The septicemic plague, with mortality close to one hundred percent of an infected population.[65]

Over the course of just seven years – from 1346 to 1353 – these plagues ravaged women and men, young and old, rich and poor, educated and illiterate, fit and frail, reducing the worldwide population by 100 to 125 million people.[66]

In Europe, the toll was particularly heavy in the urban centers which had begun to flourish across the continent. The historian Barbara Tuchman described the devastation this way:

> "In Paris, where the plague lasted through 1349, the reported death rate was 800 a day, in Pisa 500, in Vienna 500 to 600. The total dead in Paris numbered 50,000 or half the population. Florence, weakened by the famine of 1347, lost three to four fifths of its citizens, Venice two thirds, Hamburg and Bremen, though smaller in size, about the same proportion."[67]

Philip Daileader, a professor of history at The College of William and Mary, paints an equally grim picture. He cites recent research which estimates the death toll at 45 to 50 percent of the entire population in the main cities of Europe.[68]

The random, widespread and seemingly unending lethality of the Plague left European society exhausted and drenched in pessimism, fanaticism and self-indulgence.[69] Previous norms of social decorum and lawfulness were shattered, and civil constructs that had preserved at least a measure of peace and stability were destroyed. Hope for the future or even a modest confidence in the prospect of self-preservation all but collapsed.

Today, a **Melancholic Plague** is generating a similar sense of futility and despair – not physically as devastating, of course, but psychologically and emotionally just as crippling. It too is driven by a pandemic, but this plague is unlike its 14th century predecessor. It is an ethical sickness, an infection of the beliefs and behaviors of America's leaders, role models, institutions and, most tragic of all, even certain segments of its population.

As with that earlier epidemic, it is also a complex of three vicious diseases:

THE OLIGARCHICAL PLAGUE

A debilitating disease of anger and hopelessness caused by:

- business leaders who pay themselves millions even as they hold down the hourly wage of workers or simply lay them off to burnish their quarterly earnings report;

and

- an investment cabal on Wall Street and in hedge funds all over the country that encourages companies to abuse their employees or worse, to break the law or deface the planet, all to line their own pockets.

THE BETRAYAL PLAGUE

A disheartening disease of frustration and disillusionment caused by:

- a politico-governmental class that sells its votes to the highest bidder without regard to the impact their actions have on working men and women or the planet;

and

- a rogue segment of the media, law enforcement, the entertainment industry, government and other public institutions that abuses and debases women, minorities and the powerless.

THE FACTIONAL PLAGUE

An eviscerating disease of fear and insecurity

caused by:

- an unending series of conflicts among Christians, Jews and Muslims; nationalists, white supremacists and immigrants; whites and people of color; rich, poor and the forgotten; police and those they police; and straights and the LGBTQ community;

and

- the barbarism and depravity of evil terrorists who highjack religions and the despair of those lost in poverty to consolidate their power and justify the horrific acts they commit against innocent individuals and all of humankind.

The seemingly unending atrocities inflicted on people by each of these plagues have undercut the morale and sense of unity in the United States. They have spread alarm and anxiety as well as discontent and even hatred throughout the population, creating new fissures of social animosity and exacerbating old ones. America has always had its divisions and tensions, but those inflamed by these three modern-day plagues are more virulent and much more destructive.

Just as bad and maybe even worse is what happens afterward. The verbal and written echo chamber of the 24 hour news-competition-cycle as well as omnipresent social media, talk radio and cable programming extend and multiply the horror of the plagues. Meanspirited and hurtful actions replayed with endless words and commentary have coalesced into a new American melting pot. Unlike its storied ancestor, however, this pot doesn't blend us together – it boils us up to a rage.

A sampling of the headlines Americans have been forced to consume in just a single year – 2017 – illustrates this melancholic stew:

- Retired priest in western Pa. accused of child sex abuse[70]

- Five accused in D.C. to Wall Street insider trading scam[71]

- Violence. Threats. Begging. Harvey Weinstein's 30-year pattern of abuse in Hollywood[72]

- KKK members protest LGBTQ pride march in Florence· Hate 'reared its ugly head'[73]

- Matt Lauer Fired From Today After Sexual Misconduct Claim[74]

- Health care CEO gets year in prison for fraud[75]

- Anti-Muslim Hate Will March in 30 Cities This Weekend[76]

- Man Charged With Killing One, Injuring Two in Possible Hate Crime Due in Court[77]

- Orlando shooting is latest in growing trend of workplace violence, expert says[78]

- Dallas Cop Shoots Black Teen 15, In Head

With Rifle; Medical Examiner Rules Death a Homicide[79]

- Former Boy Scouts Sue Portland Chapter Over Sex Abuse Claim[80]

- Black Lives Matter shouts down 'War on Cops' author.[81]

Sadly, this situation repeats a familiar pattern of societal unrest — a time marked by events that were both the same as and different from those of today. The 1960s in America were convulsed by visceral debates and violence, protest marches and sit-ins, the destruction of property and the radicalization of ignored or mistreated Americans. Although there were several precipitating factors, the two most important were the battles for civil rights and the Viet Nam War. These conflicts inflicted deep wounds on the American public, but their pain and residual impact would have been relatively contained within specific communities had it not been for a single technological development: for the first time ever, Americans on the home front were able to see the brutality of social strife and foreign wars up close and in living color on their television sets every evening.

They could see men and women and even children being doused by water cannons and attacked by police dogs on the streets of American cities. They were forced to watch as American soldiers were ripped apart by mortar fire and ambushed by a ruthless enemy that hid behind women and children in ramshackle villages. And, they couldn't avoid the images of children's bodies carried from a bombed out African-American church or those of anti-war protestors strewn across the green of an American university.

The seemingly unending atrocities inflicted on people by each of these plagues have undercut the morale and sense of unity in the United States.

Today's reporting of our multiple, simultaneous plagues on news outlets, personal blogs and social media sites is the same kind of disaggregating agent, only on steroids. It isn't limited to our evenings at home, but instead, assaults our senses all day long. It doesn't come at us from a single local newspaper and three national television networks, but instead, batters us from a thousand points of gloom and doom. The illness itself is horrible, but this relentless portrayal of the worst of us makes it that much more demoralizing. It forces us to see the evil within and around us over and over and over again.

All of that we've done to ourselves and to make it worse, we also left ourselves open to a virtual nerve agent attack. Russia poisoned our weakened spirit with a social media advertising and trolling campaign during the 2016 Presidential campaign. In October of 2017, Facebook reported that it had uncovered 80,000 posts made by Russian-linked organizations and individuals on its site – posts that sought to deepen the distrust and discontent festering in the country – and that "mal-information" was subsequently seen by as many as 126 million Americans or almost four-in-ten citizens.[82] Even worse and more tragic, inaction by the federal government and indifference by many tech companies have permitted this virtual attack on the nation to continue unabated.

The dissention and despair brought on by our own unsanitary social habits and by the poisonous touch of malicious external agents have already maimed the lives of millions of American working men and women. They have eviscerated our People's:

- **belief in America** as the land of opportunity where everyone has a legitimate and equal shot at success through hard work and dedication;

- **trust in America** as a country committed to fairness and respect for human dignity and to the application of swift and certain justice for those who abuse their power or position;

- **onfidence in America** as a place where parents can give their kids a better life than they had, in a culture where there is a universal and revered allegiance to the common good; and

- **faith in the American Dream** and the place it calls home – a nation where the full dimension of humankind is welcomed, nurtured and celebrated.

These foundational elements of America's democracy – belief, trust, confidence and faith – have not yet died within the American population, but they are in deep distress. And, that distress will grow even more acute over the next one hundred years. The resulting weakness will challenge the Republic, but also create the conditions that will lead to a cure. Out of the suffering of the American spirit will come the courage and determination to overcome its cause – the Melancholic Plague.

Americans will not come to the Neonaissance because they have outgrown the Industrial and Information Ages – although that will certainly be true. They will step up to it because they have rejected the behaviors and beliefs of the oligarchical, betrayal and sectarian plagues. They will ask more, expect more, champion more from both themselves and from their fellow citizens. Circa 2118, Americans will enter the Age of Ennoblement because they have chosen to reinstall purpose and dignity in their lives.

THE TECHNOLOGICAL SINGULARITY

The second impetus for Americans' acceptance of the primacy of self-ennoblement is as simple as it is profound: they will have both the freedom and the wherewithal to do so. They will be lucky enough to live in an era when technology will remove their concerns about the first two tiers in Maslow's hierarchy: physiological and safety needs. These will be met by the installation of Universal Healthcare Insurance and a Universal Basic Income in America. For the first time in their history, Americans will not have to worry about their daily grind or their daily bread. The former will no longer exist, and the latter will be guaranteed.

As a consequence, the Neonaissance will be a new Act of Emancipation for all Americans. Each and every citizen will be free to pursue a form of Happiness that was simply unimaginable in the Industrial and Information Ages, and to do so, regardless of their race, creed, color or previous servitude, their national origin, sexual orientation, gender, age or disability. The imperative of employment for pay will have been eliminated for all.

Every American will have the right and the opportunity to decide how they will spend their day. They will be able to reject work altogether, but also to volunteer for whatever job they want. They can choose work that expresses their talent and engages their calling. Or, they can decide to do that and also reach for more in their lives. They can choose to devote themselves to a parallel job within themselves, one that immerses them in the elucidation of their own spirituality. The course they take will be up to them.

This economic freedom of choice will be made possible by an event called the **technological singularity**. It is not an unexpected development even today, having been predicted by researchers and futurists since the 20th century. For example, Vernor Vingne, a science fiction writer and academician, described it this way in 1983:

> "We will soon create intelligences greater than our own. When this happens, human history will have reached a kind of singularity, an intellectual transition as impenetrable as the knotted space-time at the center of a black hole, and the world will pass far beyond our understanding."[83]

While Vingne does not use the adjective *technological*, it's clear from both the context and his later writings that he was describing precisely that kind of event. The distinction is important because today there are other fields that acknowledge a singularity – gravitational studies, mathematics and mechanics, for example – and each of them uses the term in a different way. The technological singularity, however, is probably the widest known because it has been featured in our popular culture. It's starred in television shows (Star Trek: Enterprise) and in movies (in 2017), and it's been showcased in novels (in 1985 and 2004) and even in record albums (Jim Morris, Robby Krieger).[84]

Unlike today's fifteen minute fixations, the technological singularity has had almost forty years of notoriety. It's attracted this level of attention because it describes one of the most frightening developments humans have ever faced. The technological singularity denotes that point in time when machines finally and forever become more intelligent and thus more capable than people. It is humankind's ultimate Pandora's Box.

This milestone isn't just another step forward on the roadmap of technology, the latest model of this smartphone or that tablet. Rather, it is a point of existential redirection – a corner on the sidewalk of human history. When our species turns that corner, it will abruptly enter an entirely new dimension where evolution will be replaced by revolution, and where gradual development will be supplanted by rapid and accelerating, pervasive and life-altering change. The technological singularity will profoundly reshape the experience of our species on earth. And it will begin in America.

Once the technological singularity occurs, humans will no longer be the smartest creation on the planet. They will have outsmarted themselves with machines that can outthink, out-conceive, out-infer, out-imagine, out-analyze, out-evaluate, out-deduce, and out-conclude them. They will have taught these machines how to learn and then given them access to all of the data from all of human history, and all of the knowledge from all of human research and discovery. The net effect will be to grant to algorithms based somewhere in the cloud an intelligence greater than their own. When Americans round that corner, machines will be capable of creating other machines all by themselves, and those second, third and fourth generation machines can and will eventually be employed to perform every human task requiring learning, decision-making or both.

To many, that will sound like the hyper-exaggerated claims of techno-true believers. The impact on people – the tectonic shift it will impose on their lives – is simply too great to be possible. It is too utterly incomprehensible to be real or even plausible. And yet, according to many credible experts, the countdown clock is already ticking. When a group of scientists, academicians and futurists was convened in 2012 to predict the arrival of the technological singularity, their median estimate was, by historical standards, literally around the corner. They predicted it would occur in the year 2040.[85] Said another way, human life, in general, and human employment and work, in particular, will be fundamentally recast in less than two decades.

This milestone isn't just another version of technology, the latest model of a smartphone or a tablet. It is, instead, a point of existential redirection - a corner on the sidewalk of human history.

There are, of course, those who argue that such an existential reset will not or could not occur. Members of the "will not" school typically posit that no matter how different this new technology might be, its introduction in the workplace will be similar to that of other disruptive inventions in the past. It will destroy some jobs, but it will also create some too. And, when the dust settles, the number of new jobs gained will be greater than the number of old jobs lost.

Ji Shisan, the pen name for Ji Xiaochua, the founder of Guokr.com and Guokr MOOC Academy, expressed such a fingers-crossed view in *The New York Times* in 2015:

> "But history shows that employment usually recovers after a technological revolution – though the directions it can take may be unexpected. There is a lot of debate over how much disruption the AI Revolution will bring, but I am optimistic that new jobs will replace the old ones in areas we can't even imagine yet, just as the working world evolved after the Industrial Revolution. We don't blame the steam engine or tractors or sewing machines for unemployment now."[86]

Called "creative destruction," this notion was first developed and articulated by the economist Joseph Schumpeter. As he put it in *Capitalism, Socialism and Democracy* way back in 1942, economic innovation inevitably leads to a "gale of creative destruction" that "revolutionizes the economic structure from within, incessantly destroying the old one, incessantly creating a new one."[87]

While that may have explained Industrial and even Information Age economic dynamics, however, there's little evidence that it is relevant in an era of super-C machines. Indeed, at this point, the only data which exist – that drawn from the use of robots on automotive and other production lines – support exactly the opposite conclusion. That evidence makes it unambiguously clear that the introduction of artificial intelligence and machine learning technology in the workplace will destroy more jobs than it creates. It will produce higher, not lower levels of unemployment, and it will limit the employment it does offer to an ever smaller and more highly skilled cohort of the workforce.

The "could not" school of singularity deniers, in contrast, argues that society simply would not allow it to occur. The scientists and engineers who have the resources and expertise to create the technological singularity would be either self-restrained enough or, alternatively, forced by some enlightened regulatory or governmental body to stop short of or find a way around the total destruction of human employment.

The adherents to this school often cite as proof the development of nuclear technology, which did not proceed until scientists had figured out a way to contain its potentially destructive power. And yet, Three Mile Island, Fukushima and Chernobyl still occurred. Similarly, engineers, systems analysts, programmers and other IT practitioners as well as the corporate leaders who directed them launched the internet, World Wide Web and social media without first gaining an understanding of and finding a way to control the harm that could be caused by the technology. They either knowingly ignored or naively misjudged its potential use for viral and malicious personal attacks, the transmission of inaccurate or completely false information, the global spread of crime and terrorism, and the propagation of socially disruptive advertising by hostile countries.

Others in this school argue that it is illogical to think that humans would create a capability with the power to undercut their own standing in the world. The computer scientist and philosopher, Jaron Lanier, for example, has declared that "If you structure a society on not emphasizing individual human agency, it's the same thing operationally as denying people clout, dignity, and self-determination."[88] Humans are simply too smart, he suggests, to do something irretrievably stupid, and that competence will save the day.

Of course, this smiley-face view of human nature conveniently ignores the species' well documented propensity for self-destructive behavior. From slavery to tyranny, from ethnic cleansing to genocide, humans have consciously and deliberately harmed the well-being, dignity and self-determination of other humans. There is no reason to believe super-C machines would be similarly destructive – Hollywood's envisioning of Terminators notwithstanding – but they will be able to destroy human employment, and humans will happily create them to do just that.

As flawed as these arguments are, however, they both illustrate the prevailing assumption in contemporary literature about the arrival of super-C machines. Though almost never acknowledged, it accepts that the displacement of humans from employment means that they will no longer have anything meaningful or worthwhile to do with their day. Near universal unemployment will be the end of their work. Of their productive lives. Their purpose in life will be gone; their role in history will be over. As the late Stephen Hawking famously declared, "The development of full artificial intelligence could spell the end of the human race."[89]

THE TWIN PEAKS OF NOBILITY

The Neonaissance embodies the antithesis of the end-of-life assumptions about hyper-intelligent machines. Its arrival means that humans will be free to do work that accords them more self-expression and fulfillment and greater self-awareness and tranquility than they ever received from paid employment. This new era gives them the opportunity to pursue Happiness in two new and uniquely beneficial ways:

- by employing their talent in an endeavor about which they are passionate because it enables them to accomplish a worthwhile goal;

and

- by employing their need for metaphysical answers in a spiritual practice that inspires them with a deep peacefulness.

Circa 2118, Americans will enter the Age of Ennoblement because they have chosen to reinstall purpose and dignity in their lives.

THE TALENT SINGULARITY

The first of these central aspects of the Neonaissance will enable Americans to reach for nobility through their capacity for excellence. Employing themselves in work about which they are passionate and in which they can apply their talent is the single pathway to the apex of Abraham Maslow's original hierarchy of human motivation. It rejects the elitist view of talent and signals that point in time when people become more engaged with their talent than with the intelligence of machines. As such, it represents the talent singularity and opens all Americans to the only kind of employment that yields self-actualization. Achieving fulfillment through their life work will elevate their being and ennoble them as the most passionate creation on the planet.

The collection, reduction and analysis of data will continue to be important societal functions, but they will be almost entirely performed by machines. So too will research and development and scientific inquiry. Humans, on the other hand, will shift their attention and priority to the expression of their innate capacity to live life to its fullest. That activity will become the central dynamic of their education, their social interactions and their work. It will be celebrated as the means by which they advance their species, the yardstick by which they measure their progress, and the evidence they include in their history books to reinforce their superiority over machines.

THE SPIRITUAL SINGULARITY

The second central aspect of the Neonaissance will open Americans to self-ennoblement through their spirituality. By employing themselves in the search for their relation to and interaction with the divine, the sacred or the mystical, they acknowledge a twin peak of human motivation higher than self-actualization. Abraham Maslow himself recognized the existence of such a summit in his later years, calling it self-transcendence. He wrote that "Transcendence refers to the very highest and most inclusive or holistic levels of human consciousness, behaving and relating, as ends rather than means, to oneself, to significant others, to human beings in general, to other species, to nature, and to the cosmos."[90] The Neonaissance, therefore, encompasses both the talent singularity and the spiritual singularity – the moment in time when humans acquire the ability to prioritize metaphysical prowess over machine intelligence.

Such a consciousness is unique to humans. Moreover, as others have noted, humans are inherently hard wired to search for the answers to such existential questions.[91] As with our talent, its expression is idiosyncratic to each individual, but the capacity and determination to do so is a defining attribute of our species. Unlike other living creations and certainly unlike machines – no matter how capable – humans are equally curious about what they can perceive and what they cannot. They are fascinated by what can be recognized and understood with data and what data cannot define or measure. Achieving tranquility through such soul work will also elevate their being and ennoble them as the most inspired creation on the planet.

In the Neonaissance of the 22nd century, the quest for self-actualization and self-transcendence will be viewed as the norm in day-to-day life. The outcomes they produce – fulfillment and tranquility – will be recognized as unique expressions of human Life, exclusive gifts of human Liberty, and the only truly consequential milestones in the human pursuit of Happiness. They will, in effect, enable each and every person to believe in and experience their superiority over machines and their innate nobility. And, when they do, the United States will have become the world's first **noble democracy**, granting every individual the right to define and work at both their talent and their spirituality. Some will refuse to participate, but most will choose to take on this new and substantial facet of their citizenship in the country. They will see the opportunity to do their life work and their soul work as a fundamental component of being American.

Chapter 10

The Transformation Agent

"Human history becomes more and more a race between education and catastrophe."

H.G. Wells

The Ninth Amendment to the U.S. Constitution states: "The enumeration in the Constitution, of certain rights, shall not be construed to deny or disparage others retained by the people."

According to the National Constitution Center, the Supreme Court has found that these unenumerated rights include "the right to travel, the right to vote, the right to keep personal matters private and to make important decisions about one's health care or body".[92] Similarly, the Constitution is silent on the right of citizens to discover and express their innate talent. According to the interpretation of the Center, therefore, every child in America is free to find their capacity for excellence and to employ that capacity in any lawful endeavor they choose.

That view will slowly gain acceptance and in the Late Second Middle Ages, a group of parents in McLean, Virginia will organize to protest the Gifted and Talented programs in their county's elementary schools. A leader of the group, which will grow to include several hundred residents, will tell a reporter from the local television station that their quarrel was not with the Gifted and Talented program, itself, but with the resulting segregation it imposes in the classroom. They will argue that kids who are excluded from the program have as much right to their talent as the kids in the program. Their position will eventually sway the county school board, which will order the Superintendent of Schools to find a more equitable way to nurture children's capacity for excellence.

The parents, however, will not be content with their local victory, so shortly thereafter, they will establish a nonprofit organization to bring the issue to the attention of school systems across the country. They will call it MoveUp.org, to highlight their belief in every American's innate ability to elevate themselves through the application of their talent.

The situation will be very different with regard to spiritual practices. As every school child learns, the First Amendment of the Constitution does explicitly recognize the right of each person to practice whatever Religion they choose. It does not, however, similarly acknowledge their right to pursue a spiritual practice which does not consider itself or is not generally accepted as a Religion. This ambiguity will provoke the passage of hundreds of state laws and local ordinances creating a thicket of contradictions and festering disputes. Rather than leave the issue to the uncertain interpretation of the courts, the Congress will finally act and clarify the Constitution's language early in the 22nd century.

After much debate, the House of Representatives and the Senate will pass a bill which the President will sign to establish, clearly and explicitly, every American's right to engage in any form of spiritual endeavor, whether or not it is recognized by a formal name or organized by a formal canon. Not unexpectedly, that law will be tested in the courts and ultimately be reviewed by the U.S. Supreme Court.

A group of wealthy citizens in Dallas, Texas will convince the city government to ban "extreme spiritual practices" as a threat to public safety. A Mexican-American shaman – a person revered by some residents in the community as a guide to the world of spirits – will then sue to overturn the restriction. The case – Gonzales v. Dallas City Council – will ultimately become as influential as Brown v. Board of Education in the 20th century and confirm all Americans' access to any and all forms of spirituality.

This recognition of the application of talent and the practice of any form of spirituality as rights granted to every American will mean that engaging in either or both is, by definition, an expression of American citizenship. Just as with the right to assemble peaceably and the right to vote, self-actualization and self-transcendence will become two of the fundamental ways in which the country's citizens participate in their democracy. Admittedly, American citizens pick which of these rights to exercise and to what extent – the freedom to do so being itself a right – but the formal recognition of such activity as a protected right will shift the way they are addressed by the country's institutions, especially its education establishment.

AMERICA'S CURRENT EDUCATION SYSTEM

Historically, the country has accepted the solemn duty of preparing its citizens to exercise their Constitutional rights and has relied on education as its primary vehicle for doing so. Today, just as in the past, the education system tutors proto-citizens – the nation's children – on America's history and foundational principles and equips them with the knowledge and skills to live out the American Dream. It enables and empowers each child to meet the responsibilities and enjoy the privileges of American citizenship.

That will continue to be the education system's role in the 22nd century, as well, but with an important difference. Its degree structure and curriculum will be substantially revised in order to prepare young Americans for the new reality of super-C machines and near universal unemployment. They will still need to understand and respect what it means to be an American citizen – though even that curriculum will require changes – plus they will have to be immersed in a new body of knowledge and set of skills for living with intelligent machines and maintaining their superiority over them.

Currently, most Americans learn the rudiments of their citizenship in their local school. While parental guidance and role models are just as if not more important, public education has been the incubator of democratic practice in America. Kids begin each day by reciting the Pledge of Allegiance (or, if they're not citizens, listening to it) and then through classroom discussions and special assemblies, homework assignments and field trips, they acquire an understanding of how the government works, their role in directing that government, and the values and principles for which their nation stands. As with grammar lessons and quadratic equations, the knowledge isn't always fully acquired or retained, but almost every student does gain a real if sometimes subliminal appreciation for the singular opportunity and accountability they have as an American citizen.

For them to realize that opportunity, however, they also need knowledge of a different sort, and public education has delivered that, as well. From reading, writing and arithmetic – the 3 Rs – taught in village school houses in the late 18th century to calculus, physics and foreign languages taught in public high schools at the end of the 20th century, America's education system has transformed those born as citizens into actual ones. While there were other theories and concepts involved, its guiding principle was based on behavior best exemplified by the Founding Fathers. Their speeches and debates and ultimately their collective decisions – all communicated with clarity and power – established the conviction that an educated person made the best citizen.

That wisdom has shaped the curricula in America's public schools ever since. Their goal has been and remains two-fold – to develop adults who are:

- capable of understanding and critically analyzing the issues of the day and expressing their opinions about them accurately and clearly;

and

- able to earn a living sufficient to care for themselves and their families and contribute to the nation's prosperity.

In accepting and meeting those goals, the American classroom has played a singularly important role in society: it has acted as the keeper of American democracy. The importance of that lofty mission, notwithstanding, there has been no generally accepted notion of what exactly it entails, especially in recent years. Experts and educators, themselves, have debated both the format and methodology for instruction and the specific knowledge and capabilities teachers should be imparting in order for children to live out their lives as full and productive citizens.

Historically, the country has accepted the solemn duty of preparing its citizens to exercise their Constitutional rights and has relied on education as its primary vehicle for doing so.

Some argued that the focus should be on employment preparation. Public schools, they pointed out, have always been the place where students acquired the tools both to enter the American workforce (although seldom with an awareness of either their talent or their calling) and to continue their learning as necessary for their sustained employment. As they saw it, public schools taught kids how to reach for the American Dream and have done so from the country's earliest days as an agrarian society through its industrial era in the 19th and 20th centuries and into the present and the Information Age.

Others, in contrast, saw a more complex set of roles for public education. A 2014 report by the National School Boards Association (NSBA), for example, summarized an earlier report by The

Center for Education Policy which identified not one, but six distinct goals for public education:

1. To provide universal access to free education.

2. To guarantee equal opportunities for all children.

3. To unify a diverse population.

4. To prepare people for citizenship in a democratic society.

5. To prepare people to become economically self-sufficient.

6. To improve social conditions.[93]

Still others have argued that education's goal should be much more forward-looking and attuned to societal changes. A 2012 article in *Forbes*, for example, cites the view of author Daniel Pink:

"In his book, *A Whole New Mind*, Daniel Pink argues that, as a society, we have transcended the so-called Knowledge Age and are now in a Conceptual Age where our problems no longer have a single verifiable answer. Success in the Knowledge Age was mainly determined by a "SAT-ocracy": a series of tests throughout the education system that required logic and analysis to identify a single correct answer. This does not meet the needs of the Conceptual

Age, which requires creativity, innovation and design skills. He further asserts that education is still firmly geared towards the needs of the Information Age, a quickly disappearing era. It's as if our children are moving along an assembly line, where we diligently instill math, reading, and science skills and then test them to see how much they retained, making sure they meet all the "standards" of production. Today, a successful member of society must bring something different to the table. Individuals are valued for their unique contributions and their ability to think creatively, take initiative and incorporate a global perspective into their decisions."[94]

This lack of consensus among educators and social critics has been accompanied by a rising level of unhappiness with the "product" of the education system among both employers and parents. Employers point to graduates (of private as well as public schools) who lack the skills and knowledge needed in today's workplace as well as to those who have the skills but can't put them to work. Companies have openings to fill – literally millions of them – but can't find enough workers with a sound grounding in STEM subjects. Or, they have too many candidates – including those at the PhD and Masters level – who have the requisite education but can't write a grammatically correct sentence or express themselves clearly in a discussion so are unable to contribute on-the-job.

Similarly, parents point out that their investment in education for their children – now running between $110,000 and $200,000 for a Bachelor's degree[95] – has not prepared these emerging citizens for employment. They see public education as an elevator to career success and that mechanism isn't working. Their view is supported by countless stories in the media of freshly graduated young adults overlooked or lost in the job market. They are selling shoes and making skinny lattes instead of selling new ideas to management and making strategic decisions.

The reality, however, is somewhat more nuanced. Almost all college students do actually find paid work within a reasonable period following their graduation. According to Stastista, the unemployment rate for recent college graduates as of June, 2017 was just 4 percent.[96] At the same time, however, legions of parents rightly complain that their kids have to move back in with them after graduation because they cannot afford to live on their own. In effect, technology has already so reshaped the workplace that the studies young adults are pursuing to get their Bachelor's degree simply do not provide them with the necessary skills and knowledge to land a job with either a self-suporting wage or any opportunity for advancement or even continued employment.

The situation is even worse for those whose education ends with a high school degree. These young citizens have a higher unemployment rate and, when they can find a job, fill positions with much lower pay than that of their college-educated peers. According to the Economic Policy Institute, since the Great Recession of 2009, high school graduates have faced tough odds finding work and seen their pay drop three percent when they have landed a job.[97] In addition, almost a third of this population (30.9 percent) is underemployed, meaning they can only find part-time work or are so discouraged, they only sporadically look for a job.[98] They have little or no prospect of advancing into the Middle Class and no hope at all of achieving the American Dream.

As a consequence, today's secondary and post-secondary schools alike are rethinking their role. Even the report by the National School Boards Association noted above went on to state:

"In the current age of accountability and reform, the trend does seem to have coalesced around the need for a singular focus on college and career readiness—at least from the perspective of the current leaders in education reform along with federal and state government."[99]

Educators, government officials, civic oversight boards and parents alike are increasingly of the mind that education's primary role should be to prepare young Americans for (sufficiently) paid employment as adults. That's true not only in public schools but in a growing number of private institutions, as well.

For example, a new type of education "intermediary" has arisen to give students an alternative to college degree-based employment preparation. It includes bootcamp programs such as those offered by Galvanize, PrepMD, Always Hired and Ubed; staffing models such as the ones launched by Revature and Avenica; and income share agreements such as that at Mission U.[100] While each of these approaches provides a different model for employment preparation, all are private educational programs that are considerably shorter and less expensive than a traditional four-year college degree curriculum. Perhaps more important, all claim to provide exactly the skills young adults need to enter the workforce able both to contribute in a meaningful way and to do so while earning a self-suporting wage.

Collectively, the proponents of all of these schools of thought are driven by a single precept: the best way for education to prepare Americans for their role as citizens is to give them the tools to go to work. More specifically, education's mission is **employment enablement** – to set Americans up to work for someone else in jobs largely designed to benefit that other party. It is to fit them into a system where the stock market soars, companies reap record profits, CEOs and their direct reports pocket millions each year, and the median American household has seen its pay decline by 12.4 percent in just the past two decades.[101]

Nevertheless, given the economic realities of the next one hundred years, it's likely that this precept will grow even more firmly established in American society. As technology decreases the number of jobs that are available and increases the skill and knowledge requirements to perform those jobs that are available, employers and parents alike will demand more of the education system. Circa 2118, however, the two trends will intersect. When that happens, there will no longer be enough jobs to employ even the most highly educated people in the workforce. At that point – when super-C machines produce near universal unemployment – preparing citizens to work for a paycheck in jobs that exclusively benefit their employer will become and be widely accepted as obsolete.

THE SYSTEM'S NEW PURPOSE & STRUCTURE

Circa 2118, education will continue to play its central role in preparing young Americans for citizenship, but the structure and content of the country's education system will change to reflect a Tier Two Society. Advances in nutrition and healthcare will enable youth to mature physically at an earlier age. Omnipresent social media and information resources will accelerate their socio-cultural awareness. And the Neonaissance, itself, will set a higher priority on the importance of people giving back to the society of which they are a part. As a result, the federal government will lower the nation's age of maturity to 17 and require the states – where the age is now either 18 or 19 – to follow suit. It will also set the age of 17 as the threshold for full citizenship and the right to vote.

As young citizens reach that age, they will be required to register with the federal government, just as all males between the ages of 18 and 25 must do today. This requirement will apply to men and women alike and to transgender individuals, as well. The registration will have two purposes:

- First, it will automatically provide their personal information to their home state for inclusion on its official voting rolls. It will ensure that they have full and unfettered access to the ballot box.

- Second, it will mark the beginning of their 3-year period of public service to the nation. It will enable them to gain additional maturity through their contribution to important societal functions.

Each individual will be able to spend their public service commitment in an endeavor of their choice. As a 22nd century riff on the Civilian Conservation Corps and the WPA Federal Art Project during the Depression, this **citizenship practicum** will offer them a range of options, including roles in military or government service as well as public art installation; mentoring and other youth support programs; hospice and other palliative services; and care and community for the aged, the infirm and the needy. Their participation will have several goals. First, it will teach them the responsibilities of citizenship; second, it will give them their first or additional experience with working; and third, it will provide the means by which they can "test drive" their talent, their calling or both.

Upon completion of their 3-year tour of service, each person will be awarded a tuition-free education in a public institution of higher education. Having learned their responsibilities as American citizens through hands-on practice, these 20-year olds will have earned the right to the benefits of that citizenship. And, having acquired greater maturity and some insight as to the kind of work they most want to do and do best, they will be able to set an educational goal that enables them to exercise that right in their lives. It won't be true of everyone, of course, but the vast majority will use their tuition-free course of study to acquire the skills and knowledge they need to become full and engaged citizens in 22nd century America.

This new approach to citizenship preparation will maintain the central role of the education system, but require it to operate at a higher level and for a much longer period of time. Like the UHI/UBI, the cost of this expansion will be covered by the Omni Class Protection Tax and the Machine Employment Tax. As it did in creating the G.I. Bill at the end of World War II, the government will make this investment both to recognize the contribution these young citizens have already made to the nation and to help them shape a personal future worthy of that contribution.

To fulfill this update to its historical mission – to deliver the education these 22nd century citizens deserve – public colleges and universities will have to redesign both their pedagogy and their curricula from the ground up. While much of the instruction will be turned over to super-C machines, those professors who truly love teaching will still be in the lecture halls, but they will be imparting their wisdom as volunteers who are pursuing their calling. They will relate to their students in a way even the most empathetic android cannot, and they will provide a perspective on the content of their course that only a human can. As a result, the super-C machine faculty will be world class conveyors of knowledge and skills, while the human faculty will be passionate conveyors (and models) of the intellectual excitement and enrichment such learning can provide.

Other changes will transform both the structure and content of coursework and the initial degree that is awarded for its successful completion. Majors will be eliminated and the Bachelor's degree retired. Appearing for the first time during the 12th century, the word Bachelor was derived from a term used to describe a knight who was either too young or too poor to play an independent role in society.[102] By 2118, it will have become the name of a degree earned in studies of academic majors that leave many graduates similarly unable to act as full and productive citizens of the country.

During the Neonaissance, public higher education will be reimagined to correct that deficiency. It will require students to focus their studies in three Primes or areas of concentration over a period of six years in order to earn an Omnia Paratus degree – the Latin term signifying one's readiness for all things.

To fulfill this update to its historical mission - to deliver the education these 22nd century citizens deserve - public colleges and universities will have to redesign both their pedagogy and their curricula from the ground up.

The Primes will be designed to give students the three competencies required for full citizenship in America circa 2118:

PRIME #1

Coursework designed to help each person discover or confirm their innate talent – their special capacity for excellence – and to explore alternative occupations or callings where they might be able to employ it. This Prime will enable and empower citizens to work on themselves in a role that leads them to self-actualization.

PRIME #2

A course of study that introduces each person to world history and philosophy as well as religious and metaphysical studies all designed to acquaint them with the age-old quest for humankind's meaning and place in the cosmos. This Prime will help students chart their own spiritual journey and through that experience achieve self-transcendence. It will also prepare them to make an informed opt-out decision, should a spiritual experience not be right for them.

PRIME #3

A set of courses in science, technology, engineering and mathematics designed to give each person a familiarity and level of comfort with rapidly evolving machine intelligence and the omnipresence of advanced technology in society. This Prime will ensure that each citizen knows how to interact with, monitor and control super-C machines so that they are served – not intimidated, threatened or harmed – by them.

AN EXISTENTIAL CAVEAT

This education-based program for citizenship readiness will provide the intellectual, emotional and psychological infrastructure for the Neonaissance. It will be as vital to the health of the American way of life as the roads and bridges, broadband access and digital systems of the Industrial and Information Ages. It will also be equally as vulnerable. Just as America's physical infrastructure was allowed to deteriorate in the late 20th and early 21st century, so too can the country's vision of and commitment to citizenship preparation crumble in the face of indifference and neglect in the 22nd century. Americans may have a right to their talent and their spirituality, but they are not similarly guaranteed the knowledge, skills, insights and understanding required to enter the Age of Ennoblement.

There is, as a consequence, nothing inevitable about the Neonaissance. It is a possibility, not a certainty. It can happen, but it will only if Americans measure up to an irreducible challenge. For the Neonaissance to emerge, Americans will have to stay focused on their founding values and take the necessary steps to protect and express them over the next one hundred years.

For the Neonaissance to emerge, Americans will have to stay focused on their founding values and take the necessary steps to protect and express them over the next one hundred years.

It won't be easy. Or like anything they've ever experienced before. The next one hundred years – this Second Middle Ages – will be a time of constant change and widespread tumult. It will be roiled by confusion and consternation as the roles of breadwinner and careerist, even highflyer and lifer disappear. It will be filled with hardships and deprivation as machines replace humans in job-after-job-after-job. And, it will be convulsed by anxiety and fear as unemployment overwhelms entire families, neighborhoods, cities and states.

This disruptive period will cause people to question their role in society, their aspirations and dreams and even their own worth. It will shake the very foundation of the country as a whole and the futures of each of its individual citizens. Between now and circa 2118, Americans will face a test not unlike the one they faced when the nation was born. It will be – as one of the Founding Fathers described that earlier period – "the times that try men's souls."[103]

There will be those who discount such a warning as so exaggerated, it is akin to yelling "Fire" in a crowded movie theatre when no threat exists. There will be others who cluck that there is no need for alarm, that scaring people is out of place and cruel. And there will be still others who charge that the message unfairly impugns the good intentions and hard work of technologists around the world. In truth, it is none of those; it is instead simply the expression of a modern day exhortation — a trope known by all and accepted by most as appropriate and important to the times. This warning is just another way of affirming, "If you see something, say something."

But more than that, the Second Middle Ages is a doorway, a portal to a more perfect union. If the warning is heard and heeded — if America's five generations during that period step up to and realize their unique greatness — they will open the country to an era that exalts every person's life and soul. They will usher in the Neonaissance. They will lead the nation into the Age of Ennoblement.

CIRCA 2118

Chapter 11

The Age of Ennoblement

"The central question of 2025 [and beyond] will be: What are people for in a world that does not need their labor, and where only a minority are needed to guide the 'bot-based economy?'"

Stowe Boyd

The Renaissance – a period that is generally considered to encompass the 14th to the 17th centuries – is celebrated as a particularly important turning point in human history. It marked the end of the Middle Ages and the beginning of what we now call the Modern Age. No less important, the period signaled a fundamental reinvigoration in scholarship, research and aesthetics, producing an historic outpouring of artistic and scientific accomplishments.

That combination makes the Renaissance an appropriate metaphor for a similarly momentous period – the Neonaissance. It will emerge circa 2118 and mark the end of the Second Middle Ages and the beginning of the Age of Ennoblement. It too will take humankind in a new and historic direction, giving birth to endeavors that unmask people's talent and vitalize their spirituality.

Despite these similarities, however, the metaphor is an imperfect one. The two eras are as different as they are alike. And yet, it is that comparable yet divergent aspect which helps to illuminate the contours and dynamics of the new period more sharply. In effect, the Renaissance helps to confirm both what the Neonaissance is and, just as importantly, what it is not.

AN ILLUMINATING METAPHOR

While there is, as always, academic debate about the causes and central themes of the Renaissance, the majority of opinion supports the following:

- The period was shaped by the "rebirth" of classical Greek and Latin philosophy, literature and culture, beginning in Italy and then sweeping across the whole of western Europe.

- It produced a deluge of societal, philosophical, political and scientific advances that reset the human experience, including most significantly, the rediscovery and then extension of humanism, a system of thought that emphasizes realism and reason, observation and evidence.[104]

- The goal of humanists was to leverage research, data, analysis and logic "to create a universal man whose person combined intellectual and physical excellence and who was capable of functioning honorably in virtually any situation."[105]

- While the period saw the patronage of scholar-princes produce some of humankind's greatest artistic accomplishments, the most important cultural development was the replacement of feudal relationships with commercial ones, enabling broad segments of society to achieve occupational independence and the ability to pursue their own fortunes and dreams through paid employment.

The Neonaissance, in contrast, will begin in the 22nd century and have an even more consequential impact on human society, economics and culture.

- The Neonaissance will be a "new birth" of human endeavor and exploration, not a rediscovery of ideas and values from the past. The era will open in the United States and then sweep across Europe and the rest of the developed world from there.

- It will produce a vast expanse of societal, philosophical, political and scientific developments that reset the human experience, replacing its exclusive focus on humanism and advances derived from rationalism and reasoning with a binary perspective that includes an equal commitment to the perfection of individual work and advances derived from self-actualization and self-transcendence.

- The goal of this movement will be to leverage all learning and metaphysical inquiry to create a "noble person." Each individual will be encouraged, empowered and enabled to commit themselves to two endeavors: first, to identify their unique capacity for excellence and determine where best to employ it so as to achieve a deep and durable fulfillment and second, to connect with the infinite, the sacred or the awe-inspiring and answer for themselves humankind's timeless spiritual questions so as to achieve a profound and lasting tranquility.

- While figures of great nobility will emerge during this period and their individual acts and accomplishments will fill the pages of post-22nd century history books, the most important cultural development will be technology's elimination of all nonvoluntary employment and the replacement of labor-based compensation with a Universal Healthcare Insurance and a Universal Basic Income program that frees every American to define and reach for their own noble destiny.

Being human, of course, can be described in many ways, but in most cases, the depiction reduces to four aspects of experience: physical, mental, social/emotional and spiritual. The entirety of our existence – from our first to our last waking moment each day – involves one or more of those aspects. Collectively, they encompass all that we are, and just as important, they represent what is unique about the human species – an elemental differentiation which has been the source of our dominance on the planet since we learned to walk upright. That will not change circa 2118.

Machines can and will mimic one or two of those aspects – they will be built with strength and taught (or teach themselves) mental prowess – but they cannot be fully social/emotional or in any way spiritual. Only humans can be those ennobling aspects. The way we will do so in the Neonaissance, however, will differ significantly from the way we do so today. If we are to remain the planet's superior creations, we will have no choice but to infuse all of those aspects into the way we work and, as a result, change the purpose of employment and our role in it.

Most people consider work to be an integral and natural part of the order of things. We devote our adulthood to it, and then – at least in the 20th and so far in the 21st centuries – we retire from it. But always, it is the metronome of what we "do" during our day. Work – good, bad or indifferent – is as central to our being as our need for oxygen. It alone provides an effective way to meet those tier two physiological and safety needs in Maslow's hierarchy.

Work, however, is not the same as paid employment. In fact, it wasn't until the Renaissance that people freed themselves from feudal indenture and began to enter into agreements to lease their capabilities to others who needed work to be done and were willing to pay for its completion. That implied or actual contract enabled vast swathes of the population to meet their tier two needs – to care for themselves and their families – and gave them a way to broaden what they saw, learned and understood. It provided a place where they could tap into the physical and mental aspects of their being and even, in some cases but to a very limited extent, into the social/emotional aspect, as well. Certainly, there were other activities that also touched those aspects, but paid employment consumed so much of their waking day, it had far-and-away the greatest impact.

In the Age of Ennoblement, that will no longer be the case. Machines will perform almost all work – at least work as it has traditionally been defined – so paid employment will no longer be available. Americans will have lost that platform for expressing the physical and mental aspects of who they are. They will, as a consequence, have to find another way to be themselves – to live as the unique human they are – and, at the same time, to preserve their dominance on Earth. Ironically, they will discover this new conduit in the two aspects of their existence that work has seldom if ever touched: the social/emotional and the spiritual. Humans will continue to work, but with their tier two needs met, they will be free to do so in a way that lets them engage with those aspects that complete their humanity. That totality of being, in turn, will ennoble them and reinforce their position at the apex of the evolutionary pecking order.

E NOBILIS UNUM

The Age of Ennoblement will not signal either the advent of an aristocracy or the dawning of the Age of Aquarius in America. It will not mean that Americans have accepted a rigid class structure in their culture, their politics, the business world or any place else. Or that they will set themselves up as modern-day Henry David Thoreaus and retire to solitary contemplation in the words. This new age will not recognize the legitimacy of capitalist oligarchs or the domination of religious radicals and zealots. And, it will certainly not announce Americans' acceptance of a karaoke standard in human affairs or their intention to live as saints.

So, what then will this momentous epoch – a period that will carve out its own special place in history – portend for the American people? How will it shape the culture in which they live? And, what will be its impact on their lives – on their relationships and passages, their aspirations and prospects?

When considering any era in the human story, it's easy to be captivated by the headlines. We dwell on the period's famous figures and major events and seldom pay much attention to the way the general population lived their lives. We overlook the humdrum of daily affairs and, instead, focus on the period's scientific discoveries and new inventions; the work of its artists and authors, musicians and poets. We ignore the conversations and concerns of "ordinary" people and memorize the debates among its politicians and social critics; the teachings of its religious leaders and philosophers; and the wartime exploits of its admirals and generals.

In large measure, this focus on the extraordinary is due to the tenacious sameness of human nature. While any historical period is unique and important for both its improvements in living standards and the impact of its milestones, the banalities of the past were much like those of the present. The everyday ups-and-downs of people's lives – their passages and relationships, their routines and habits – have been largely unchanged throughout the years, and it is that sameness which makes those lives seem unremarkable and unnoteworthy.

Even in a period as extraordinary as the Renaissance, the reality of life for most people was much more mundane and far less memorable than the lives of the period's great figures. Filippo Brunelleschi, Leonardo Da Vinci, Sandro Botticelli and Michelangelo Buonarroti were the striking exceptions to the general rule. For everyone else, life was unremarkable and ... well, ordinary.

Their days unfolded, each in its own unexceptional way with happy times and disappointments, the marking of birthdays and anniversaries, and the daily chores. They witnessed the expression of humankind's finest attributes and feats, yet also endured long days at work, dealt with unruly children and rebellious teenagers, and worried about debts and obligations that never seem to end. While humanism may have celebrated our species' intellectual and creative gifts, the people of the time were just as tired, irritated, befuddled and stressed as those who preceded them.

The same will be true for Americans living circa 2118. Breathtakingly capable technology will transform their homes and hometowns into oases of comfort and convenience, but their interactions with others – their spouses and partners, children and grandchildren, relatives and friends, acquaintances and strangers – will still be complicated. They will have more free time than ever before and greater freedom to apply it as they wish, but they will also experience daily routines that are just as mundane, engage in quarrels that are just as petty, and live through situations that are just as engaging and exhilarating, disconcerting and irksome as they are today.

The Neonaissance, however, will also have a gray underside that is unlike anything experienced in previous periods. The cultural shock of no longer having to hold down a job to put food on the table and a roof over one's head will disorient and disaffect a not inconsequential segment of the population. Some will feel overwhelmed and frightened by the loss of a supportive structure and goal for their day. Others will fall into a profound sense of emptiness and despair that they will try to dispel with alcohol or drugs or even self-abuse. And, still others will sink into a kind of stupor, seeing the freedom from employment as an invitation to do nothing at all, to sit at home and binge watch artificial or farcical lives on television.

Most people consider work to be an integral and natural part of the order of things. We devote our adulthood to it, and then - at least in the 20th and so far in the 21st centuries - we retire from it. But always, it is the metronome of what we "do" during the day.

Happily, however, the rest of the population – and that will be the majority – won't be similarly affected. They will be able to adapt to this new reality and take a different tack. They will see near universal unemployment as an opportunity to do whatever it is they have always wanted to do, but because of their paid employment obligations, could not. What was once a sporadic pastime will now be their full-time occupation. What was once a daydream – something they could only imagine doing if they had a fortune in the bank – will become the mission that shapes their daytime. Their daily grind for someone else will be transformed into their daily adventure with and for themselves. Remarkable will become a characteristic of every person's life — extraordinary will be democratized.

For some, this shift will be the first time they've ever been able to devote as much time as they would like to a cherished avocation or hobby. They may compete in a favorite sport or test themselves with a physical challenge. They may pursue their love for astronomy or gardening or spend their time fishing or making music with a band. They may work at building kids' character through scouting or get up on stage as the member of an amateur acting troupe. There will be no project deadlines or office crises, no badgering bosses or demanding customers limiting what they can do. They will be free at last to engage in whatever activity gives them enjoyment and a sense of satisfaction.

That enjoyment and satisfaction, however, does not equate to the fulfillment and sense of accomplishment a person achieves through self-actualization. Indeed, as Maslow and others have noted, achieving the feeling of having done something significant with one's life is a high order human need. It is one of our species' strongest and most compelling motivators. For that reason, many and maybe even most Americans will eventually revert to some form of working. They will miss the pressure of deadlines or the collegiality of co-workers or the tiredness they used to feel at the end of a long workday. In the Neonaissance, however, they will be seeking something more – something that eclipses their standard of living, something that enhances the quality of their existence. And, to achieve that outcome, they will work in a completely different way than they did in the past.

Thanks to the UHI/UBI, they will not need paid employment, so they will volunteer to work and do so only for organizations they admire. They will set the terms of their commitment and structure the role they play. In a very real sense, they will employ themselves, applying their capacity for excellence to work that enables them to achieve self-actualization and the fulfillment and sense of accomplishment it produces.

In addition, today's focus on an organization's human resources and human capital will give way to an individual's search for "organizational value." More and more people will subject their employer to an annual "engagement review" to ensure it continues to provide them with a worthwhile work experience. Should that ever cease to be the case, they will pack up their talent and take it to a higher quality job with another organization. Circa 2118, however, such new roles will no longer be seen as an organization's "employment opportunities," but rather as an individual's "talent contribution." The jobs will not be something employers provide if and when it benefits them, but rather something persons of talent accept if and when it serves their needs and goals.

But, what work will they do? If companies are almost entirely automated or operated by super-C machines, exactly what contribution will humans be able to make?

In a consumer-based economy, many organizations will bring in human talent to express their value proposition to the public. Just as celebrity endorsements give today's products and services credibility and cache, human endorsements will do so for machine-generated products and services in the future. Humans will also be used to test and review new products and to assess the strategy for branding them in the consumer marketplace. They will serve as the "humbundsman" when machines cannot adequately resolve customer service issues, as "humoralists" who counsel an organization's machine leadership on the direction of its research and development, and as "humenders" to help organizations repair their brand after a commercial misstep or failure.

Additionally, humans will flock to nonprofits that provide social services for the needy, homeless, aged, sick and infirm. They will revel in their use of skills in which they excel and for which they have been trained – as doctors, lawyers, information technologists, teachers, logisticians, truck drivers and more. They will employ their talents in organizations with missions in the U.S. and in those with missions that take them to other countries around the world. They too will revel in the execution of tasks that contribute to an outcome they see as meaningful and worthwhile. They will choose to work, not because they have to but because they want to.

All of these and other similar endeavors will be present in the Neonaissance, but they will not be its sole defining ethos. Talented contribution and accomplishment will be central features of the period, but they will not be the only way we think about or characterize it. Instead, this new era will also be defined by its focus on human spirituality and the exploration of the soul. This additional dynamic will inspire a new form of work that is equal in importance to the work people do with their talent. In effect, every American will have two jobs in their pursuit of Happiness: one that taps their mind and heart and rewards their work in the world with self-actualization, and a second that taps their mind and soul and rewards that work within themselves with self-transcendence.

The former will provide a way for them to find and experience their special capacity for excellence in the workplace. The latter will enable them to answer the fundamental questions at the very core of human existence:

Why am I here?

Where did I come from?

What is my place in the universe?

How do I give my life value and meaning?

The shape and content of these two jobs will be idiosyncratic to each individual. They will select them, define them, implement them and derive their own understanding of Happiness from them. The fact that they can do so is the most important distinguishing feature of the Neonaissance. Unlike in the Renaissance or any other period in history, for that matter, there will be near universal access to what scholars will record and celebrate as the substance and sweep of the era. Those with "ordinary" lives no less than the period's celebrated figures will be able to participate. Not everyone will join in, of course, but most will, not just because they can, but also because they recognize or at least subliminally sense the heretofore unattainable benefit it confers. The installation of the Universal Health Insurance/Universal Basic Income program will enable and empower each and all of them to explore the essence of themselves – to become more aware of and in touch with the entirety of what distinguishes them as a human being. To achieve nobility.

Talented contribution and accomplishment will be central features of the period, but they will not be the only way we think about or characterize it. Instead, this new era will also be defined by its focus on human spirituality and the exploration of the soul.

While this elevation of the role of talent will be welcomed and celebrated, the parallel elevation of spirituality will be controversial, at least to some. They will see it as the opening that inevitably leads to the establishment of a state religion. Their fears will be misplaced, however, as the country's commitment to the separation of Church and State will remain intact. Unlike in other countries where religion plays such a role, America will not reset itself as a theocracy – "a form of government in which God or a deity is recognized as the supreme civil ruler, the God's or deity's laws being interpreted by the ecclesiastical authorities."[106] Rather, America will continue to revere its tradition of government of, by and for the people, but embed within that political system a culture that also cherishes their spiritual diversity.

That multiplicity of expression will be seen as an unalienable Right, a 22nd century comprehension of the First Amendment to the Constitution. While legal scholars have long debated what is and is not covered by the word "religion," Americans have effectively interpreted its meaning for themselves. Since the earliest days of the Republic, they have freely practiced whatever formal religion or spiritual conviction they chose.

Even in the early decades of the 21st century, when tensions rose over the acts of terrorists who claimed to be Muslim, most Americans refused to demonize those who practiced that religion. They saw themselves, instead, as sibling communities of faith and peacefully worshipped as Christians, Jews, Buddhists, and Hindus and – yes, as Muslims too. In fact, they defined their familial relationship in the broadest of terms so that it also included those who devoted themselves to spiritual movements that were outside the boundaries of mainstream religions, including those described as New Age, Native American, Wiccan, Pagan and Druid.[107] Circa 2118, the federal government will finally catch up with society and explicitly interpret the Amendment's reference to religion to mean that broader definition. It will declare that "Congress shall make no law respecting an establishment of religion or other spiritual practice."

The Neonaissance, therefore, will harness the lifeless and soulless power of super-C machines to liberate Americans from involuntary paid employment. It will not be a proclamation, but instead, the animation of emancipation, freeing them to pursue the ultimate dimensions of Happiness, however they choose to define that end. It will unleash their native talent and their inherent spirituality to elevate each and every man and woman to the pinnacle of their being. As that fulsome citizenship emerges in the 22nd century, America will retire its historic description as the "land of opportunity" and reimagine itself as the even more uplifting "land of self-ennoblement."

AMERICA AS A
NOBLE DEMOCRACY

Circa 2118, a profound shift will occur in the way people see themselves and their relationship to super-C machines. When they exercise their right to work at both their talent and their spirituality, when they reach for those uniquely human summits of motivation and need – self-actualization and self-transcendence – they will live out their superiority over all machines:

- They will have accomplished tasks that machines cannot perform – life and soul work,

and

- They will have achieved states of being human that machines cannot learn or emulate – fulfillment and tranquility.

As a consequence, people will elevate themselves to a singular status on the planet. They will open the Age of Ennoblement by ennobling themselves.

The rank or social status of nobility has been a feature of human activity for centuries, of course. Its pinnacle was probably during the Middle Ages, when the way nobility could be achieved was actually studied and debated in Europe.[108] The primary school of thought conceived of ennoblement as the product of an individual's exemplary habits and deeds. Although often intertwined with classical and Christian views of what constituted "exemplary," it was fundamentally a celebration of a person's work in the world and the beneficial results that work achieved. Further, as Wikipedia explains, "Geoffroi de Charny, the noted celebrant of knighthood, argued 'God will mark out those who labor valorously, even though they come of little estate' (*Livre de chevalrie*, in Oeuvres de Froissart, ed. K. de Lettenhove I, pt. iii, 494, 495)."[109] In other words, even though later traditions limited the achievement of ennoblement to an aristocratic class, its original conceptualization envisioned it as a rank to which anyone could aspire and everyone could reach through exemplary work.

In reality, however, access to the rank was constrained because it could only be conferred by a higher power. Anyone might be able to do exemplary work, but it would only ennoble them if God or a monarch acting on God's behalf decided it was worthy of being so recognized. While nobility could (and still can) be inherited, the title was, in practice, always originally derived from a Sovereign and in recognition of a person's service to the crown.[110] In England, for example, the Duke of Cornwall, the Duchess of Sussex, and the sixth Earl of Grantham all received their titles from the King or Queen.

Such a notion was the antithesis of the principles on which the American democracy was founded. Indeed, the U.S. Constitution (Article 1, sections 9 and 10) specifically prohibits the conferring or inheriting of a noble title.[111] That prohibition is a legal one, however, and aimed at the European conceptualization of the term. In America circa 2118, ennoblement will not be an indication of social status, but instead be a measure of human dignity. It will, therefore, both follow and diverge from the original European notion.

The Neonaissance, therefore, will harness the lifeless and soulless power of super-C machines to liberate Americans from involuntary paid employment.

Like its European cousin, American ennoblement will be a rank that can be achieved by anyone. That doesn't mean the country will become a monarchy with an aristocratic class – the rise of princes and princesses among today's oligarchs notwithstanding – but that it will, instead, evolve into the world's first noble democracy. In America circa 2118, nobility will be an attribute of, by and for the people.

Unlike in Europe, however, American ennoblement will not be conferred by a monarchical power but rather by the person, him or herself. They will achieve that distinction by demonstrating a contemporary definition of exemplary habits and deeds. In other words, the status will be realized via personal acts that lead to the attainment of uniquely human summits of being – self-actualization and self-transcendence. Those summits, in turn, will produce uniquely human benefits – personal fulfillment and tranquility – that deepen their appreciation for their species and establish its superiority over even the most intelligent machines.

The work required to attain those summits

and produce those benefits simultaneously leverages and expresses an individual's talent and their spirituality. They are the exemplary habits and deeds of democratic nobility.

TALENT

Despite the word's frequent usage in American business and culture, talent is widely misunderstood in America today. Even the dictionaries offer definitions that are open to misinterpretation. Merriam Webster, for example, defines talent as "a special often athletic, creative, or artistic aptitude."[112] Similarly, Dictionary.com defines it as "a special natural ability or aptitude."[113]

In truth, talent is the natural or inherent capacity to excel, but it is not "special," if that adjective is meant to suggest that talent is something possessed only by extraordinary people. On the other hand, talent is special if the adjective describes a superlative human characteristic that can be uncovered and nurtured by everyone. In effect, talent is a universal aptitude that deserves democratic recognition. Each and every person has a talent, and circa 2118, they will at last acknowledge that fact and act on it.

The way that recognition occurs in the Neonaisance will reflect two, fundamental truisms about talent:

TALENT IS SOMETHING
HUMANS LOVE TO DO

The dictionary definitions of talent are correct, of course (with the caveat regarding the designation of "special"), but only as far as they go. In truth, talent is actually composed of two elements: it is the inherent or natural capacity for excellence, and it is something that people love to do. That second element of the definition is every bit as important as the first. It elevates humans over machines – those inanimate creations are unable to feel any emotion, let alone passion – and it differentiates the expression of one's talent from the simple albeit superior performance of a function.

Since the dawn of the Industrial Age, most Americans have been going off to work without any knowledge of their talent. Over the course of their career, however, they often acquire the expertise and experience to do high quality work on-the-job. That superior performance, however, is not necessarily an expression of their talent, and in fact, often is not. Doing well in whatever career field or industry they stumbled into after school is, at best, a hit-or-miss way of finding that special attribute. They may come to like what they do, they may even feel pride in their work, but they are seldom passionate about it. They are what business organizations consider an asset – they are diligent, hard-working and deliver superior results – but they are not working at what they love to do. No matter how much they are paid, therefore, they cannot earn fulfillment, so most of the benefit of their effort goes to their employer.

While passion is a precondition for reaching fulfillment, however, it is not sufficient to produce that state in a person. It is a complement of, but not the whole of their talent. A person can be passionate about playing golf, for example, but as hordes of weekend duffers illustrate, they seldom have the talent to be employed at the game. Therefore, passion must be accompanied by the capacity for excellence to be a genuine expression of talent. It is a person's application of the best of themselves to tasks they love to perform. Activity that involves only one of those two elements can be enjoyable (when on the links, for example) or satisfying (when on-the-job, for example), but it cannot be fulfilling. Merging those two elements, on the other hand, is a capability only humans have, and doing so is the initial metric of self-actualization.

TALENT IS BEST EXPRESSED WHEN EMPLOYED IN ONE'S CALLING

The final metric of self-actualization is achieving a sense of accomplishment at work. Attaining that outcome is possible only when a person employs their talent in their calling. As is the case with talent, a calling is also an expression of passion. When associated with a person's talent, it is their love for achieving certain outcomes or objectives. They have a talent for leadership, for example, so love to organize and direct others in achieving an objective and excel at doing so. Their calling, in contrast, is their passion for contributing to a specific mission or outcome. Regardless of whether they make that contribution on their own or through an organization, they view it as intrinsically meaningful and worthwhile. While a calling is often associated with religion, the arts, medicine or even a particular sport, it can also be the drive to help remediate poverty, to teach young children, to build a successful business or even to keep a city's parks clean. No calling is superior to or better than another, as all callings feed people's need to feel as if they've done something constructive and valuable with their work.

Historically, most Americans have not worked at their calling because either they didn't know what it was or the occupations it involved paid too little for them to meet their tier two needs. America has a well-worn footpath from its educational institutions to jobs and employers that do little to engage or reward workers beyond giving them a paycheck. Even if they are aware of their talent and bring it to work with them, what they are actually employed to do does not involve their calling and thus fails to give them any sense of accomplishment. They put in their time, but are unable to feel as if they've expressed the best of themselves. It's no surprise, therefore, that an August, 2017 Gallup poll reinforced the findings of numerous prior surveys and reported that seven-in-ten Americans hate their job.[114]

The introduction of the UHI/UBI and the reimagination of the nation's education system in the Late Second Middle Ages will solve that problem. For many Americans, it will represent the first time they are able to go to work in a role that draws on their talent in an endeavor about which they are actually passionate. They will be employed where they can make a difference in the world – however they define that outcome – so they will push themselves to overcome challenges, find solutions and contribute to the best of their ability. They will, in effect, be expressing their capacity for excellence in their calling. As Dr. Shelly Provost, a partner in an angel investment firm that focuses on female-led startups, puts it, "A calling is passionate and compulsive. It starts as an inkling ('I'd like to try that') then swells into a mandate that you just can't shake."[115] It is, in a very real sense, the **life work** of an individual. And, accomplishing it is its own reward and the final step to self-actualization.

SPIRITUALITY

Spiritualty is, at its core, a democratic ideal. It is something to which everyone can aspire and which everyone can achieve. Circa 2118, it will also be expressed democratically as a form of work. Some will implement it as a quest, others as a journey; some will reach for it through private devotion or introspection, while others will practice their faith in the canon and fellowship of an organized religion. Some will achieve it by building a personal connection with the divine or the mystical, while others will do so by working to perfect their own being or to eradicate injustices perpetrated on humans by humans.

This work will also be guided by the emergence and acceptance of two fundamental precepts:

SPIRITUALITY IS A CORE ELEMENT OF HUMAN NATURE

The search for some higher meaning or purpose in one's life is a human attribute as important to our wellbeing as our need for oxygen. In fact, the word spirit is related to the Latin word *spirare*, which means to breath. It should not be surprising, therefore, that researchers have found spirituality to be more widespread in America than participation in a formal religion. According to a 2017 Pew Research Center survey of Americans' views on religion, for example, better than half of the respondents (54 percent) described themselves as religious, but over three-quarters (75.5 percent) considered themselves to be spiritual. Even among those who described themselves as religious, almost nine-in-ten (89.9 percent) also saw themselves as spiritual.[116]

Regardless of their personal approach to spirituality, however, most Americas share a common goal in working at it: they aspire to feel the tranquility that comes from learning about and accepting one's connection to the sacred, divine or mystical. They want to understand as best they can their own answers to humankind's metaphysical questions. And, they want to be comforted by the certainty that there is a creator of, a force in or a dimension to the universe that is more powerful than any creation humans might devise.

It is a paradox, therefore, that spirituality is actually a manifestation of human superiority on Earth. It elevates humankind by acknowledging that every person – from the most celebrated in society to the most "ordinary" of citizens – can establish a relationship (which they select) with the most powerful entity or feature in the cosmos. Further, by also providing a way for them to realize that relationship, spirituality opens humans to experience a state of being – tranquility – that only humans can achieve. It is their doorway to self-transcendence, and circa 2118, they will be able to walk through it.

THE QUEST FOR AND EXPRESSION OF SPIRITUALITY INVOLVES BOTH INNER AND OUTER WORK

The one absolute truth of spirituality is that there is no single way to arrive at it. In fact, there is not even a single accepted definition for the word.[117] Its expression by individual men and women is as diverse as they are. The Neonaissance, therefore, will define spirituality, not as a single, rigidly structured activity, but as a self-selected, inspirational occupation that consists of not one, but two distinct kinds of work. It will involve a person's work within themselves to find answers to humankind's metaphysical questions and work beyond themselves to apply those answers in service to others and the planet.

Just as they will commit themselves to their talent and calling, Americans living in the Neonaissance will also center their career on a second but non-traditional form of human work. It will be neither employment-based nor done in a profession, craft or trade. Instead, the centering will apply their intellect, curiosity and fascination to an endeavor best described as **soul work**.

This refocusing of human labor will fundamentally restructure our workday. From the moment we learned to stand and walk erect, we had no choice but to devote most if not all of that time to meeting our tier one and tier two needs. We were hunters and gatherers, then farmers and shop owners, assembly line workers and organization men and women. Regardless of the way we worked, the goal was always the same: earn enough to feed, clothe, shelter and secure ourselves and our families. Once the UHI/UBI is enacted, however, that will no longer be necessary. Americans will be able to spend their workdays fully involved in the exploration and appreciation of their soul. They will have the time, the means and the freedom to exercise the metaphysical dimension of their citizenship.

That inner work will be simultaneously extended and deepened by an equal commitment to outer work – work done voluntarily for the benefit of others. Steven Pinker wrote in his 2015 book *The Better Angels of Our Nature: Why Violence Has Declined*, that "The doctrine of the sacredness of the soul sounds vaguely uplifting, but in fact is highly malignant. It discounts life on earth as just a temporary phase that people pass through, indeed, an infinitesimal fraction of their existence ...."[118] During the Neonaissance, most Americans will come to recognize such a potential fallacy and strive to avoid it. They will conceive of soul work not as a free pass on the problems of the real world, but as an endeavor that produces tranquility through both introspection and paying it forward. Violence, prejudice, abuse, pollution and environmental damage will all still exist circa 2118, so the quest for spirituality will be seen as an obligation to confront and correct them. Soul work will open people to self-transcendence by addressing the harms that humans themselves have imposed on humankind and on their planet as well as by empowering them to reach for a relationship with their better angels.

—————————————————————————

The Neonaissance will be an historic epoch because it positions the most capable technology ever devised as an enabler of humans – as the means by which they will achieve the full measure of being human. It will not be a brave new world, but instead, **a better new world**. It will not empower super-C machines to enslave people, but instead, employ them to empower people to live and work in the Age of Ennoblement. When this new era opens circa 2118, Americans will be granted their rights of talent and spirituality as well as the means to exercise them in their pursuit of Happiness. It will be the birth of an entirely new dynamic for their day and a redefinition of the American Dream.

Chapter 12

What We Must Do

"When faced with a radical crisis, when the old way of being in the world, of interacting with each other and with the realm of nature doesn't work anymore, when survival is threatened by seemingly insurmountable problems, an individual life-form – or a species – will either die or become extinct or rise above the limitations of its condition through an evolutionary leap."

Eckhart Tolle, *A New Earth: Awakening to Your Life's Purpose*

How will America open the Neonaissance? How will the nation move from where it is today to this new era and do so by circa 2118? Consider this:

> It is not possible to avoid the challenges of the next one hundred years. It is possible to overcome them.

> It is not possible to eliminate the disruption the period will cause in people's lives. It is possible to moderate the impact of that disruption.

It is not possible to prevent the Second Middle Ages. It is possible to prepare for them.

There is no regulatory mandate or social consensus that will magically deter the development of artificial intelligence and machine learning in the near or longer term. It cannot be legislated into oblivion. It won't be prevented by the sudden onset of restraint among technologists. And, it will not be curbed by humankind's logic, compassion or anger. The introduction of super-C machines into all aspects of human life is now locked into history's irrepressible flow. It has become an integral part of the nature of things.

People are going to lose their jobs. By the tens of millions. No matter how skilled or educated or experienced they are, they will be escorted out of their permanent, full time positions and then out of their temporary, part-time and gig jobs. They will be unemployed, not in transition. They will have zero prospects for paid reemployment. Not because the economy has turned down – it will boom – but because there is nothing left for them to do in the workplace.

To protect ourselves in the face of this disruption – to manage the course of human events as it unfolds in the Second Middle Ages – each and all of us will have to adopt a new and multifaceted mission. First, we will have to recognize the life-altering crisis that is now overtaking us. We will have to find the confidence and wisdom to see the new reality of work clearly and accurately. Then, we will have to embark on new tasks that are unprecedented in terms of both what they will demand of us and the ways in which they will touch our lives. And finally, we will have to marshal the courage, the energy and the will to shape the new reality to our benefit and that of our children and grandchildren. We the People of today's USA – Boomers, Gen-Xers, Millennials and Gen-Zs – will have to step up and become the next Great Generations of Americans. Our defining test and our legacy will be to take the nation through the Second Middle Ages and into the Age of Ennoblement beyond it.

Every one of the actions we will have to take to prepare ourselves and our families for what's ahead should have at least one of three goals:

TO LESSEN THE POTENTIAL FOR SURPRISE AND TI IE PARALYZING FEAR IT CAN GENERATE.

Allowing the rise of super-C machines to arrive as a bolt-out-of-the-blue is an abrogation of our responsibilities as both adults and citizens and an invitation to expose ourselves and our families to hope-quashing misery and despair.

TO SEE THROUGH THE UPHEAVAL AND RECOGNIZE THE POSSIBILITIES AND OPPORTUNITIES BEING CREATED.

Allowing the rise of super-C machines to overwhelm us with inaction and hopelessness will close off both ourselves and our families to the positive outcomes and extraordinary benefits the new reality can also deliver.

TO LAY THE GROUNDWORK THAT WILL OPEN THOSE POSSIBILITIES AND OPPORTUNITIES TO EVERYONE.

Allowing ourselves to be surprised and paralyzed by the advent of super-C machines will leave us and our families without the perspective or preparations required to turn the next one hundred years into a doorway to an exhilarating new era in America.

These actions must be taken by each of us individually as well as by formal and informal groups and by governmental, academic and other institutions in the country. Some can and should be implemented immediately. Others will likely take years or even decades to accomplish. Some will seem obvious and even mundane, while others will require an extraordinary leap of imagination. Some will cost nothing, but demand great determination and fortitude. Others will be more expensive than any other program in the history of the nation.

The beginning of this proactive campaign, however, will be humble. It will not be the opening move of a grand strategy formulated by the federal government. It will not be launched as a bill in Congress or a doctrine of some future Administration. It will not be a plank in the platform of this or that political party or be touched off by an advertising campaign paid for by some political action committee or special interest group. No, the first step will have to be taken by We the People. Preparing for and then responding to the arrival of the Second Middle Ages can only begin with and come from each individual one of us.

There is no regulatory mandate or social consensus that will magically deter the development of artificial intelligence and machine learning in the near or longer term.

Nota Bene: The individual acts, collective actions and federal initiatives presented below are not meant to be an exhaustive list of those required for the nation to negotiate the Second Middle Ages successfully. They are provided, instead, to illustrate the scope and scale of the initiatives we will have to implement.

INDIVIDUAL ACTS

The first and most important act for each of us will be self-education. We can no longer assume that centuries will pass before the arrival of super-C machine technology, but must instead, educate ourselves on its current state and possible future directions – in the next decade and the next twenty-five years as well as in the next century. Then, we must make continuing that education a priority in our lives. Not as something we do on occasion or when it's convenient, but as a task we perform each day, every day. And, not as the New Year's resolution that gets overtaken by events, but as a permanent, life-long commitment. We must pay attention and stay attentive, whether we're a Boomer or a Gen-Xer, a Millennial or a member of the Gen-Z generation.

In one respect, however, there's nothing new in calling for such a commitment. The notion of continuous education as a strategy for workplace security has been an important theme in career counseling since the late 20th century. Unlike continuing education, which has long been a central component of many professions – from medicine to law, engineering to public accounting – continuous education denotes both a more rapid and uninterrupted pace of learning than was traditionally the case for most people and an activity in which almost everyone should be involved, regardless of their occupational field.

The first and most important
act for each of us will
be self-education.

During the Industrial Age, the knowledge and skills required to perform adequately on-the-job evolved slowly, so what it took to enter an occupation was well known and the additional learning it took to stay current could be acquired in the vast majority of occupations at a relatively lei-surely pace. Then, the Information Age dawned and jobs became infused with technology, which made them both more complex and more unstable. The power of technology was doubling every two years, so the knowledge and skills human workers needed to do their jobs with that technology also changed at the same pace. To keep up (and keep themselves employed), workers had no choice but to commit themselves to continuous education.

Even as the Information Age enters its final days, those of us in the workforce can no longer consider a degree from an educational institution or a certificate from a training program as the conclusion of our occupational learning. Rath-er, in today's and tomorrow's technology-dense workplace, it is simply the beginning of what we must know if we're to be employment-ready. We have to accept that – no matter our occupational field, level of expertise or length of experience – we are now never complete or completely done. We must act as if we are a "work in progress" be-cause, in fact, in the new world of work, we are.

That is challenge enough for most of us, but the arrival of super-C machines has added a mandato-ry new dimension to our continuous education cur-riculum. Not only must we stay abreast of the ev-er-changing requirements in our profession, craft or trade, but now we must also pay attention to what advancing AI and machine learning technology is doing to the workplace, in general, and to our field of work and industry and our job and hometown, in particular. We must, in effect, achieve and then maintain situational awareness. Even with the most up-to-date occupational skills and knowledge and even if we are a so-called "A level performer," we are vulnerable to job loss if we aren't equally as adept at recognizing and preparing for the introduction of ever-greater numbers of byte-collar workers.

That doesn't mean we need to acquire the ability to program algorithms or create data taxonomies or develop neural networks. Situational awareness doesn't involve teaching machines how to think like humans or to understand the vagaries of human speech. Rather, it is the process of proactively searching out, analyzing and adapting as necessary to the impacts those developments are having on the world around us. We have to figure out, based on the best available information, how our work and workplace are being affected, in the present, the near-to-mid-term, and in the years beyond that.

Admittedly, this additional requirement does make continuous, work-related education a much more complex endeavor than ever before. It requires that we tap a broader range of sources and points of view than those upon which we have traditionally relied for career security and that we immerse ourselves in communities and educational experiences that may be uncomfortable or even intimidating, at least at first. We will have to learn a new vocabulary, wrestle with unfamiliar and es-

oteric concepts, and confront ideas and their consequences that seemed unimaginable just a few
years ago. And, we will have to do all that while
still investing the time and energy required to stay
at the state-of-the-art in our occupation and job.

Some will undoubtedly ask why we should both-
er, given everything else we have to do in our lives.
It's a reasonable question, but one with an unknowable answer since the causal event – machine hegemony in the workplace – will not yet have occurred. The best explanation, therefore, is a simple
if somewhat crude analogy. The acquisition of situational awareness is similar to the steps we take
to protect ourselves when walking down a deserted
street at night in an unfamiliar neighborhood. Paying attention to what super-C machines are doing
in the Second Middle Ages is just another way of
scanning the sidewalk in front of us, looking back
over our shoulder from time-to-time and staying
alert to sudden movements in the shadows. It's a
reasonable and prudent precaution to take when
what lies ahead is unknown and potentially hostile.

Situational awareness, therefore, isn't a crys-
tal ball-like prediction of the future, but instead it is a way to **machine-proof our careers**
as they unfold. It is an educated assessment of
the shape and direction of a new reality in the
world of work in order to optimize – as much as
is possible – our position and wellbeing in it.

We can, of course, turn to formal academic programs that cover the subjects of artificial intelli-

gence, machine learning, natural language processing, deep learning, neural networks and the like.
Such instruction can be found at both public and
private institutions, ranging from the University
of Tennessee-Knoxville, the University of Califor-
nia-Berkeley and the University of Washington to
Carnegie Mellon, MIT and Stanford University.
Some courses are taught at the undergraduate level,
others at the graduate level and still others through
continuing education or certificate programs.

What is true of almost all of this instruction, however, is that it addresses topics related to how to build
super-C machines and work with their constituent
technologies. It is developed and taught by the faculties and staff of Machine Learning Departments,
Artificial Intelligence Labs and Schools of Computer & Information Science. While such courses
are clearly appropriate for those seeking a career in
those areas, however, they do not help the rest of us
achieve situational awareness. The instruction focuses on providing the skills and knowledge to develop and apply the technology, not on the information and insights to assess and manage the impact
of those developments and applications. Therefore,
in academic institutions at least, a more useful perspective is likely to be gained in the faculty departments that oversee the Business curriculum and
select courses in Human Resource and Workforce
Management. Not all such departments offer courses on how to work along side super-C machines, but
some do, and those that don't are likely to do so

as that work arrangement becomes more prevalent.

There are also credentialing and other training programs offered by commercial or professional organizations, ranging from Udemy's *Artificial Intelligence A-Z*™ and Coursera's *Deep Learning for Business* to SAP's *Machine Learning in Financial Services: Changing the Rules of the Game* as well as the International Institute of Information Technology's course on the *Foundations of Artificial Intelligence and Machine Learning.* Some of these courses and those offered by similar organizations are taught in person and some are offered online or through a self-study format. Some require the payment of a fee, while others are offered at no cost.

A third and less formal source of situational awareness is, of course, those in the workplace. It's hard to say how many people are now at work on and with the technology, but undoubtedly it is in the tens of thousands worldwide. Through their employment in corporate labs and research centers, they are often the closest to the workplace advances being achieved in and with artificial intelligence. They may be conducting that research or supervising it; they may be promoting the resulting products in the marketplace or selling them to potential customers. Regardless of their role, however, they often bring a unique perspective that blends the exploration of what the technology can do and the introduction of its applications in commercial and other settings. In short, they're the ones who are reshaping our jobs with super-C machines.

We can acquire at least some of the lessons they're learning by listening to their podcasts and reading the business and technical publications to which they contribute. We could, for example, listen to *Talking Robots*, produced by the Laboratory of Intelligent Systems at EPFL in Switzerland or read the publications posted by the Natural Language Processing Group at Microsoft. Similarly, we can join the online discussion groups in which these subject matter experts participate and even attend the conferences where they speak. We might, for example, visit the Artificial Intelligence News blog at ScienceDaily.com or attend the O'Reilly Artificial Intelligence Conference or the Summits held by Singularity University.

Other sources of information and opinion that can help advance our situational awareness include:

Professional societies and trade associations.

For example, SHRM – the Society for Human Resource Management – has published articles such as "Artificial Intelligence Can Boost HR Analytics, But Buyer Beware," while the Signal Processing Society at IEEE – the Institute of Electrical and Electronics Engineers – has published "The Future of Productivity: AI and Machine Learning."

General media, including blogs, magazines and newspapers.

For example, *The Huffington Post* published an

essay entitled "AI in the Workplace: Preparing for the Fourth Industrial Revolution," while *CMO* from IDG, a publication for Chief Marketing Officers, published a story on its site about "What AI will do to the future of work and how humans do their jobs."

Researchers and expert commentators.

For example, Tobias Baer and Vishnu Kamalnath from McKinsey & Company published a piece entitled, "Controlling machine-learning algorithms and their biases," while Shelly Palmer, the former host of a TV talk show and a blogger on technology, opined about "AI: 5 Things Every CEO Should Know."

Regardless of the sources we use, the key to gaining useful situational awareness will be our ability to separate fact from fiction and bias from impartiality. Unfortunately, there is already a hype bubble developing in some quarters of the AI industry, and that can make it difficult to know what's real and legitimate and what's hyperbole and hucksterism. In addition, even subject matter experts are influenced by the assumptions they make and the circles in which they travel so their views can also be unintentionally (or not) slanted one way or another. In the early years of the Second Middle Ages, therefore, each of us will have to vet the source of any content we encounter and proactively search for alternative views that may help to provide a more balanced and thus accurate perspective.

As more and more of us educate ourselves on

the looming challenge posed by super-C machines – as we gain situational awareness – we will also recognize the importance of supplementing what we do for ourselves with actions we take for our collective benefit. The disruption will be too great, the challenges too enormous to deal with individually, and as each of us comes to realize that, we will accept the need for collaborative action. Sadly, this realization won't generate a universal response – there will be those who refuse to acknowledge their responsibility to participate – but for most, it will be as compelling a call to our common defense as any we've experienced as a nation.

COLLECTIVE ACTIONS

As important as our individual preparation will be, it will fall far short of what the country will need to negotiate the Second Middle Ages successfully. To do that, we will have to couple those personal acts with collective actions. We will have to act as individuals and take action in groups.

As de Tocqueville noted in his writings about America, our citizens – more than those of any other country – are joiners.[119] We revere the right of peaceable assembly, not simply as a platform for debate and the expression of political opinion, but as a launching pad for collective action.

In some cases, that action can and should be developed and implemented by formal groups –

groups with elected or appointed leaders, defined structures and established budgets. It might, for example, be channeled through a political party or through a civic action group such as the Southern Christian Leadership Conference, a public policy advocacy group such as MoveOn.org, or a consumer advocacy group such as the Center for Auto Safety. [Sadly, a similar advocacy group for people required to work with super-C machines does not currently exist.] Typically, these groups use a range of actions to advance the interests of their members, including lobbying at the state and federal level, media campaigns, research and the publication of policy statements or proposals.

In other cases, however – and they are likely to be the most prevalent over the next one hundred years – it will be up to America's citizens to lead the effort by joining together in informal groups. This role is a familiar and fitting one. Americans have always coalesced around important issues – from the Suffragettes fighting to give women the right to vote to Everytown for Gun Safety working for stricter gun control laws. In nationwide movements and neighborhood committees, such informal groups have mobilized, marched and protested so their concerns would be heard by their fellow citizens and their government. In many respects, these groups are the purest form of democracy. They enable every citizen, regardless of their social station – employed or unemployed, housewife or househusband, old or young, professional or tradesperson, point.1-percenter or hourly worker – to assemble, organize and direct themselves to meaningful action.

The #MeToo movement is a perfect case in point, It exemplifies the power of such informal groups to change public perceptions of and tolerance for individual or group misconduct. The issue it addresses was one that had festered for far too long in the country at large and the workplace, in particular: sexual assault and harassment, especially directed against women. Though used previously by a social activist, a single tweet by just one woman in 2017 propelled the hashtag into a worldwide movement that has challenged the behaviors, policies and leadership of businesses large and small; local, state and federal governments; political, academic and athletic institutions; and the media. It has called out movie stars and moguls, athletic coaches and trainers, corporate executives, Members of Congress and those who tolerate or abet their predatory behavior. It has, in short, democratized the disgust at and condemnation of sexual misconduct regardless of where it occurs and who perpetrates it.[120]

As important as our individual
preparation will be, it will fall
far short of what the country will
need to negotiate the Second
Middle Ages successfully.

That kind of collective action is now needed to protect humans from being mistreated by the mass introduction of byte-collar workers over the next one hundred years. Americans will have to both assemble new informal groups and activate existing formal groups in a wide range of venues to ensure they know:

- How and where machines are entering the workplace and workforce;

- What changes to specific occupations, jobs, industries and locations are being caused by their introduction;

- When, where and how new and more capable machines will be added to the workplace and workforce in the future; and

- What governmental, academic, social and civic organizations are and will be doing about it.

These groups might include:

The members of professional societies and trade associations.

These groups should establish and prioritize those initiatives that will provide situational awareness in their field and the proactive development of educational and support programs that will help keep members employed until the federal government implements an appropriate national response. They should demand that these initiatives provide an accurate, real time portrait of how their profession, craft or trade is being affected as well as the trend and time lines for future impacts, and include remediation programs that are continuously updated and refined to ensure they deliver the maximum possible benefit to the membership.

The alumni of colleges and universities.

Informal groups should mobilize to demand that their alma maters be more forthright about the workplace value of their degree programs and that this information be provided to both prospective and current students. In addition, they should call for the institutions to be more directive in their expectations of faculty members, so that tenured professors no less than adjunct instructors research the impact that super-C machines are having on their area of expertise and integrate that research into their course materials. In addition, they should also mandate that all course descriptions include a certification indicating when the research was last updated.

The members of social and civic organizations, such as fraternities and sororities, veterans organizations, ethnic clubs and fraternal lodges.

These groups should accept responsibility for keeping their members and the local communities where they live informed about the pace and extent of super-C machine introductions. They should require the organizations to establish an internal research function or license the research of an appropriately accredited external organization to acquire and distribute up-to-date insights and information both in regular communications and at their national meetings, conventions and conferences.

The members of churches, synagogues, mosques, temples and other religious institutions.

These groups should establish programs that will help their institutions deal with the familial and social disruption that will accompany near universal unemployment and prepare their community for the opportunities and responsibilities that will emerge in the Neonaissance. In addition to helping their members and others who have been forced into financial distress and homelessness, these institutions will probably have to take the lead in addressing the psychological and emotional harm that continuous unemployment can inflict on adults as well as the anxiety and fear that parental calamities can cause among children.

The residents of local neighborhoods, towns and cities.

Informal groups should mobilize to demand that their leaders and governing bodies establish and prioritize programs for the collection of data on the impact of super-C machines on local employment and the needs of those who are affected; the monitoring of that data and the exploration of alternative programs to remediate adverse impacts within the community; and the creation of agencies and/ or programs to provide assistance as needed by local residents and families. The availability of such support should be continuously promoted on social media, at public meetings and in the local press.

The employees of companies of all sizes, including both those that are publicly traded and privately owned and those that are foreign based and domestic.

These informal groups should establish Company Watch initiatives similar to the Neighborhood Watch programs in their hometowns. Their mission will be to ensure transparency and accuracy in company reports detailing the installation and use of super-C machines and any resulting layoffs, whether or not they meet the thresholds established by the Worker Adjustment and Retraining Notification Act of 1988. That Act only affects employers with "100 or more employees (generally not counting those who have worked less than 6 months in the last 12 months and those who work an average of less than 20 hours a week) and only requires that they provide at least 60 calendar days advance written notice of a plant closing and mass layoff that affects 50 or more employees at a single site of employment."[121] Company Watch groups, in contrast, will mobilize to monitor all layoffs at all companies that are caused by the introduction of super-C machines and to provide timely notice to those employees and communities that are likely to be affected.

These and other collective initiatives must have two parallel agendas. The first, as described above, is to energize America's natural associations in a wide range of campaigns to prepare for and then deal with the disruption of the next one hundred years. The other, equally important agenda must be for these informal and formal groups to exert pressure on the federal government to recognize the problem and take steps to redress it. This democratic activism must be seen as neither progressive nor conservative, Republican nor Democrat. Rather, it should reflect the interests and concerns of each group's membership and be accomplished in whatever way makes the most sense for that group.

Indeed, no perspective is too parochial and no action is too modest to be worthwhile, because it is their cumulative impact that is needed. The hard truth is that, while individual acts and collective actions will be critically important, they will be insufficient by themselves to meet the challenge of growing unemployment and social disruption. Taken together, however, they will administer the "shock to the system" that can jump start the federal government and put it into action. And that action – the enactment of national initiatives with appropriate scope, authority and funding – will be essential to preserving and protecting the

American people during the Second Middle Ages.

FEDERAL INITIATIVES

Having revolted against a tyrannical monarchy, the Founding Fathers created a system of separation of powers in the new United States of America to ensure no one branch of government – executive, legislative or judicial – could amass a potentially dominating level of control. Through a series of checks and balances detailed in the U.S. Constitution, the system prevents any part of the government from being able to impose its will on another part of the government or, more importantly, on the people. In addition and to limit the authority of the federal government as a whole, the framers of the Constitution also stipulated that it could only exercise those specific powers granted to it by that document, and assigned all other roles to the individual states.

The first of these specific or enumerated powers provides that:

> The Congress shall have Power To lay and collect Taxes, Duties, Imposts and Excises, to pay the Debts and provide for the common Defense and general Welfare of the United States; but all Duties, Imposts and Excises shall be uniform throughout the United States.[122]

This clearly specified responsibility to provide for the "general Welfare" will form the basis for the initiatives the federal government must undertake in order to deal with the escalating disruption in the country during of the Second Middle Ages. Near universal unemployment will impose grave financial hardships, cause widespread homelessness, and inflict deep emotional and psychological trauma on the American people. The turmoil and harm inflicted will be every bit as severe and widespread as that of our most eviscerating crises in the past – the Civil War, World Wars I and II, and the Great Depression.

While all three of those national challenges generated effective national responses, the New Deal legislation and programs enacted in response to the Great Depression provide a particularly useful guide for the role the federal government will have to play. Its defining circumstances are the most similar to those the American people will experience over the next one hundred years:

- The Great Depression began during a time of great national prosperity – the so-called Roaring 20's. Ownership of the era's latest technology – cars, refrigerators, irons and washing machines – was widespread in the population and the standard of living had improved for most people in rural America as well as the country's cities.[123]

Similarly, a strong economy just prior to and during the Early Second Middle Ages will promote widespread employment and enable most Americans to purchase the latest technology of their era. Ownership of late model cars and SUVs, smartphones and headphones, tablets and e-readers and big screen and smart TVs will become a reality for a majority of American families, causing better than eight-out-of-ten Americans (81 percent) to rate their standard of living as satisfactory in 2015.[124]

• The Roaring 20's came to an abrupt and crippling halt with the stock market crash of 1929. In just four years, from 1929 to 1933, unemployment in the country rose from 3.2 percent to almost a quarter of the entire workforce (24.9 percent). In some locations, it reached 80 percent.[125]

Today's general prosperity will collapse with the arrival of the technological singularity during the High Second Middle Ages and the resulting replacement of ever-growing numbers of human workers with super-C machines. Within four decades, near universal unemployment will push a majority of American families to the brink of poverty.

• The despair during the Great Depression was so deep and widespread that civil authority began to crumble. Cities and towns saw stores looted and street brawls between citizens and the police and other civic authorities. Protest marches became commonplace as did shanty towns of displaced and dispossessed workers. By the early 1930s, many political and business leaders feared the country was headed to revolution.[126]

Social unrest will rise during the Second Middle Ages as the federal government struggles to understand and respond to the disruption caused by super-C machines. Fueled by the instant connectivity of social media, the largest protest marches in American history will take place in Washington, D.C. and other major cities. Congress will initially be paralyzed, and the population will roil with frustration and anger at its inaction, leaving the country teetering on the brink of chaos.

There will, however, be one stark and defin-ing difference between the Great Depression and the Second Middle Ages. In the 1930s, the econo-my tanked; in the 21st and 22nd centuries, it will boom. The earlier period saw manufacturing out-put decline by 54 percent and construction spend-ing sink a whopping 78 percent.[127] During the next one hundred years, corporate productivity growth will be the highest on record, fueling an unprece-dented rise in company profits and a bull stock mar-ket that will push all indices to breathtaking new highs … if the federal government is able to de-sign and launch initiatives that protect the general

Welfare and the wallet of the American consumer.

The New Deal legislation and programs enacted in response to the Great Depression provide a particularly useful guide for the role the federal government will have to play.

What does it need to do? The initiatives launched by the Administration of President Franklin Delano Roosevelt provide a useful road-map. They had two goals that encompassed an array of supporting programs, including:

Providing income security and meeting basic needs.

The government put Americans back to work by introducing:

- The Civilian Works Administration to accomplish infrastructure repair and development projects in towns and cities.

- The Public Works Administration to undertake major infrastructure development projects such as dams, airports and highways throughout the country.

- The Federal Project Number One of the Works Project Administration to support the creative work and performances of musicians, artists, writers, actors and directors.

- The Civilian Conservation Corps to provide unskilled young men with manual labor jobs in rural lands owned by federal, state and local governments.

Preserving social stability and individual wellbeing.

The government promoted confidence and a sense of security by introducing:

- The Federal Deposit Insurance Corporation to protect the hard-earned savings of Americans and make the use of banks safe for all.

- The Federal Home Administration to help families buy and keep their homes.

- The Securities and Exchange Commission to prevent speculation and other market abuses that were thought to have been the original cause of the stock market crash.

- An array of programs such as Old Age Assistance, Aid to the Blind, and Aid to Dependent Children to provide support for those in need.[128]

This sweeping response had both the scope and the scale to settle the country's rattled nerves, stabilize its major institutions, and provide for the general Welfare. The federal government of the 22nd century will have to do no less.

It will have to provide income security and meet the basic needs of its citizens and preserve social stability and individual wellbeing as the country transits the Second Middle Ages. Indeed, its challenge may well be even greater as the crisis facing the country will touch almost every single American and every single village, town and city in the nation.

In the years ahead, as it was in the 1930s, only the federal government will have the requisite authority as well as the resources and expertise to mount a suitable response and find a pathway through that time to a better future. Unlike the New Deal, however, its response will have to be a **New Pact** – an agreement of, by and for the People that provides the vision and commitment to remake their nation.

Among the steps it must include are:

TO IMPROVE PUBLIC AWARENESS & UNDERSTANDING

Inter-Branch and Agency Collaboration

Given the unprecedented scope of the potential disruption, all three branches of the federal government should establish a joint Special Working Group to monitor the situation on a continuous basis, assess its impact on individuals and locales, and identify legislative needs, legal issues and agency programs and regulations that will be needed to preserve the "general Welfare" as super-C technology spreads in the American workplace.

In particular, this working group should explore how best to design and introduce the only two programs capable of ensuring the continued good order and wellbeing of individuals as near universal unemployment approaches reality: Universal Healthcare Insurance and a Universal Basic Income. Further, it should be required to report out its findings and recommendations publicly on a twice-a-year basis, so the American people know what is being done – or not – on their behalf.

Data Collection & Dissemination

To keep those in the workforce and the American public, in general, aware of the spread of super-C machines in the workplace, the Bureau of Labor Statistics in the Department of Labor should begin tracking and reporting on the number of human jobs lost to super-C machines each year and year-over-year by industry and occupational category. The results should be published on the agency's website for all to see.

In addition, both the Senate and the House of Representatives should charge their appropriate oversight committees to include the rise of super-C machines in their hearings with Executive Department representatives. These hearings should be open to the public and broadcast on CSPAN to maximize the availability of the information that is provided and the visibility of the policy and programmatic responses that are debated.

Regulatory & Judicial Review

The Department of Labor should monitor employment trends to ensure that the introduction of super-C machines does not disproportionately affect any single group as defined by sex, age, race, color, religion, physical or mental disability, creed, national origin, veteran status, sexual orientation, genetic information, gender identity, or gender expression. No group should be forced to bear a disproportionate share of the impact, whether that occurs intentionally or not.

No less important, Justices on the Supreme Court should speak out on the important role the legal community will play as the country deals with the rise of super-C machines. They should encourage judicial scholars to research and debate the issues that are likely to arise as American society, business and culture deal with the ensuing disruption. For example:

- Can a human worker be required to train the machine that will replace them on the job?

- Who's at fault if a machine engages in prejudiced or biased behavior on-the-job – the developer that programmed the machine or the organization that employed it?

- Can a store be held liable for injuries a machine inflicts on a human shopper if the human intentionally confused or misdirected the machine?

- Is a marriage between a human and humanoid a legal union, and if so, does the machine have the same rights as a human spouse?

TO EDUCATE & PREPARE
THE WORKFORCE

Federal Programs & Initiatives

Executive Departments should design, fund and implement new programs to address the changing needs of the American people. For example:

- The Department of Education should develop machine literacy materials for distribution to elementary and secondary schools.

- The Department of Health and Human Services should develop bridge healthcare programs (until the UHI is passed) to provide support to individuals who have lost their jobs due to the introduction of super-C machines.

- The Department of Labor should modify the unemployment insurance program (until the UBI is passed) to provide bridge support to those workers who have no opportunity for reemployment due to the introduction of super-C machines.

- The Department of Commerce should study ways to protect byte-collar workers from compromise through hacking or malware inserted by a foreign government or terrorist organization.

In addition, the Congress should pass the Truth in Education Act, requiring all colleges and universities – as a condition of receiving any form of federal funds – to report machine impact trends by academic major to all current and prospective students. This report should specify jobs lost to super-C machines annually and year-over-year for those occupations that typically attract the graduates of each academic department. Similar to federal guidelines for the labeling of food products by manufacturers, this bill will ensure that students know exactly what they're buying and thus its potential impact on the health of their career.

Further, the federal government should acknowledge the central role that Human Resource Departments will play in ensuring employers' fair and equitable treatment of workers who are affected by the introduction of super-C machines. To that end, it should invest in the expansion of HR curricula at both the undergraduate and graduate level in higher education institutions and support the development of more advanced courseware for mid-career and senior professionals at SHRM (the Society for Human Resource Management) – the country's foremost professional society for HR practitioners and leaders – as well as other groups serving HR and related professionals, including the Association for Talent Development, the National Human Resource Association and the International Public Management Association for Human Resources.

In addition, the government should invite these groups to bring their members before appropriate agency working groups and Congressional committees to provide real-time insights on how workers are being affected on the ground. This testimony should be supplemented with input from academicians, bloggers, commentators and researchers in the HR field.

Policy Study & Formulation

All three branches of the federal government should collaborate on determining the U.S. position on the plethora of new issues created by the rise of super-C machines. For example:

- Do machines have rights similar to those enjoyed by humans? If so, what are those rights and what is the appropriate way to protect them?

- Should the development of autonomous weaponry – super-C warriors or Terminators – be banned by international treaty the same way that poison gas is now? If so, how can such a ban be enforced and who will do the enforcing?

- Should humans be allowed to turn life-or-death decisions over to a machine? Should they be permitted to authorize machines to decide when life support should terminate or even to end life at a person's direction?

The one hundred year interval required to install and adjust to a fully automated economy and society can be a period of chaos and confusion. It can permit the development of harmful as well as helpful technology and the introduction of that technology at a pace too fast for humans to understand or accommodate. It can paralyze our social, cultural and political institutions and leave us without the anchors we depend on in our lives. It can cause the disintegration of accepted norms of human behavior and lead to violence and bloodshed. It can knock the most powerful nation on Earth to its knees, making it vulnerable to hostile geopolitical forces and terrorists around the world. It can deteriorate the future for our kids and grandkids and for their kids and grandkids, as well. The Second Middle Ages – a blink of history's eye between the Industrial and Information Ages and the possibility of the Neonaissance – can be all of that. Or not. It's up to us.

Epilogue

In 2017, the novelist Dan Brown introduced another thriller entitled *Origin*. While the tale is packed with action and intrigue, it is also a provocative meditation on humankind's age-old search for the answers to questions only humans can appreciate:

- Where do we come from?

and

- Where are we going?

At one point in the book, a key figure makes this pronouncement about super-smart and capable machines:

> "These lifeless species evolved almost exactly as if they were living – becoming gradually more complex, adapting to and propagating in new environments, testing new variations, some surviving, others going extinct. A perfect mirror of Darwinian adaptive change, these new organisms had

developed at a blinding rate and now made up an entirely new kingdom – the Seventh Kingdom – which took its place beside Animalia and the others. It was called: *Technium*."[129]

That claim, of course, is fiction. There is no super-C machine species. At least, there isn't today.

Given the accelerating pace of technological development, however, there will be. It is a certainty. An inevitable new reality in America. And, it raises two more questions only humans can appreciate:

- Where will technologists take our workplace and country?

and

- Where will the rest of us fit into the future they create?

In one hundred years — **circa 2118** — we'll know the answers ... and equally as important, so too will our kids and grandkids.

End Notes

1. Kathleen Elkins, The 20 jobs that robots are most likely to take over, Business Insider, May 29, 2015.

2. Uwe Hennig, The rise of machines and AI in retail, ITProPortal, July 27, 2017.

3. Raymond Kurzweil, The Law of Accelerating Returns, 2001, Nature Physics, Lifeboat Foundation, undated.

4. Shona Ghosh, One of Europe's most influential investors gave a brutal example of how AI could wipe out white-collar jobs, Business Insider, June 13, 2017.

5. Sarah Knapton, Robots will take over most jobs within 30 years, experts warn, The Telegraph, February 13, 2016.

6. Murad Ahmed, Davos: Smart machines set to transform society, January 20, 2016.

7. Kevin Kelly, Better Than Humans: Why Robots Will – And Must – Take Our Jobs, Wired.com/gear, December 24, 2012.

8. Reference.com, Business-Finance, retrieved January 20, 2018.

9. Harriet Taylor, AI will eliminate 6 percent of jobs in five years, says report, CNBC,

September 12, 2016.

10. Stowe Boyd, When Robots Take Over Most Jobs, What Will Be the Purpose of Humans?, HuffPost, undated.

11. Daron Acemoğlu, Pascual Restrepo, Robots and jobs: Evidence from the US, VOX, April 10, 2017.

12. Wolf Richter, How Many Jobs Do Robots Destroy? Answers Emerge, WolfStreet.com, March 29, 2017.

13. Associated Press, Robots Replacing Human Factory Workers at Faster Pace, Los Angeles Times, February 10, 2015.

14. David Rotman, The Relentless Pace of Automation, MIT Technology Review, February 13, 2017.

15. Steve Goldstein, A majority of Americans make less than $20 per hour, MarketWatch, November 17, 2014.

16. Erik Sherman, 5 white-collar jobs robots already have taken, Fortune February 25, 2015.

17. Charlie Kingdollar, The Speed of Disruption and Impact on Business - The Fourth Industrial Revolution Has Begun, GenRe Publications, April 2017.

18. Richard Waters, Technology: Rise of the replicants, Financial Times, March 3, 2014.

19. Ghosh, June 13, 2017.

20. Quentin Fottrell, When Bill Gates and Mark Zuckerberg sound the same dire warning

about jobs, it's time to listen, MarketWatch, July 7, 2017.

21. Martin Ford, Guess who's coming for your job, CNN Techonomics, November 10, 2014.

22. The New York Times, SportsWednesday, September 6, 2017, p. 8.

23. Robin Lloyd, Robots Could Replace Teachers, Live Science, July 16, 2009.

24. Paul Solman, Should We Fear the 'End of Work'?, PBS NewsHour, July 3, 2013.

25. Abraham H. Maslow, Hierarchy of Needs: A Theory of Human Motivation, Amazon Digital Services, January 2011.

26. Marilyn Geewax, The Tipping Point: Most Americans No Longer Are Middle Class, NPR The Two-Way, December 9, 2015.

27. Bing.com, Spirituality, retrieved January 22, 2018.

28. Lawrence Mishel and Jessica Schieder, CEO pay remains high relative to the pay of typical workers and high wage earners, Economic Policy Institute, July 20, 2017.

29. Ibid.

30. Wikipedia, Cognitive dissonance, retrieved October 8, 2017.

31. Bing.com, Life, retrieved January 19, 2018.

32. Wikipedia, Soul, retrieved January 24, 2018.

33. David Sze, Maslow: The 12 Characteristics of a Self-Actualized Person, HuffPost-The Blog, December 6, 2017.

34. Mark E. Koltko-Rivera, Rediscovering

the Later Version of Maslow's Hierarchy of Needs: Self-Transcendence and Opportunities for Theory, Research, and Unification, Review of General Psychology, Vol. 10, No. 4, pp 302–31.

35. Andrew Sullivan, Trump's First Year Has Been a Disaster. Here's Why I Have Hope., New York Magazine, January 5, 2018.

36. Fluent LLC, Consumer Perceptions of AI, November 27, 2017.

37. Wikipedia, Middle Ages, retrieved November 5, 2017.

38. Ibid.

39. Ibid.

40. Maureen Dowd, Elon Musk's Billion Dollar Crusade to Stop the AI Apocalypse, Vanity Fair, March 26, 2017.

41. OpenAI.com, retrieved November 5, 2017.

42. AI-Austin.org, retrieved November 5, 2017.

43. Ariana Eunjung Cha, Thought Process: Building an Artificial Brain, The Washington Post, September 30, 2015.

44. Tom Ward, Google's New AI Is Better at Creating AI Than the Company's Engineers, Futurism.com, May 19, 2017.

45. Aaron Smith & Janna Anderson, AI, Robotics and the Future of Jobs, Pew Research Center, August 6, 2014.

46. Ibid.

47. Aimee Picchi, The robot revolution will take 5 million jobs from humans, MoneyWatch

January 18, 2016.

48. Jenny Awford, Will YOUR Job Still Exist in 2025?, DailyMail.com, November 8, 2014.

49. Binyamin Applebaum & Jim Tambersley, With Red Tape Losing Its Grip, Firms Ante Up, The New York Times, January 2, 2018, p A1.

50. Patrick Gillespie, U.S. has record 6 million job openings, even as 6.8 million Americans are looking for jobs, CNN Money Stream, June 6, 2017.

51. John Zappe, Temp Staffing, Freelancing: Both Growing Rapidly, TLNT, October 25, 2017.

52. GlobalFirepower.com, 2017 United States Military Strength, retrieved January 2, 2018.

53. Bureau of Labor Statistics, Economic News Release: Union Members Summary, January 26, 2017.

54. Robin Throckmorton, The 'Gig' Is Up! The Gig Workforce That Is, Strategic HR Inc, May 1, 2017.

55. Elaine Pofeldt, McKinsey Study: Gig Economy Workforce is Bigger Than Official Data Shows in U.S., Europe, Forbes, October 10, 2016.

56. Aaron Smith, Pew Research Center – Internet & Technology, Public Predictions for the Future of Workforce Automation, March 10, 2016.

57. Staffing Industry Analysts, US staffing

market to increase 3% in 2017, SIA forecast says, April 13, 2017.

58. Rana Foroohar, Saving Capitalism, Time, May 23, 2016 pp 28-31.

59. Ibid.

60. Nathan Heller, "If Animals Have Rights, Should Robots?, The New Yorker, November 28, 2016.

61. Quentin Fottrell, July 7, 2017.

62. Ibid.

63. Wikipedia, A Purpose Driven Life, retrieved April 1, 2018.

64. Jerusalem Post, Stephen Hawking: There is No God, September 28, 2014.

65. New World Encyclopedia, Black Death, retrieved September 30, 2017.

66. Saylor Academy, online course content, Black Death, Saylor.org, retrieved November 12, 2016.

67. University of Wisconsin – Green Bay, The Disastrous 14th Century, online course content, retrieved September 24, 2017.

68. Philip Daileader, The Late Middle Ages, audio/video course produced by The Teaching Company, 2007.

69. Wikipedia, Consequences of the Black Death, retrieved October 25, 2017.

70. Mark Scolforo/The Associated Press, Retired priest in western Pa. accused of child sex abuse, WITF, July 25, 2017.

71. Kevin McCoy, Five accused in D.C. to Wall

Street insider trading scam, USA Today, May 24, 2017.

72. Monica Hesse and Dan Zak, Violence. Threats. Begging. Harvey Weinstein's 30-year pattern of abuse in Hollywood, The Washington Post Style, October 14, 2017.

73. Connor Sheets, KKK members protest LGBTQ pride march in Florence: Hate 'reared its ugly head', AL.com, June 13, 2017.

74. Billy Perrigo, Matt Lauer Fired From Today After Sexual Misconduct Claim, Time, November 29, 2017.

75. Robert Patrick, Health care CEO gets year in prison for fraud, St. Louis Post-Dispatch, September 21, 2017.

76. Dean Obeidallah, Anti-Muslim Hate Will March in 30 Cities This Weekend, Daily Beast, June 9, 2017.

77. Chris Fuchs, Man Charged With Killing One, Injuring Two in Possible Hate Crime Due in Court, NBC News, February 27, 2017.

78. Christal Hayes and Paul Brinkman, Orlando shooting is latest in growing trend of workplace violence, expert says, Orlando Sentinel, June 5, 2017.

79. Tanasia Kenney, Dallas Cop Shoots Black Teen 15, In Head With Rifle; Medical Examiner Rules Death a Homicide, Atlanta Black Star, May 1, 2017.

80. Oregon Public Broadcasting Local News/

Associated Press, Former Boy Scouts Sue Portland Chapter Over Sex Abuse Claim, October 4, 2017.

81. Rick Moran, Black Lives Matter shouts down 'War on Cops' author, AmericanThinker.com, April 7, 2017.

82. Nancy Scola and Ashley Gold, Facebook: Up to 126 million people saw Russian-planted posts, Politico, October 30, 2017.

83. Richard Dooling, Rapture for the Geeks: When AI Outsmarts IQ, New York: Crown, p. 88.

84. Wikipedia, Singularity, retrieved December 5, 2017.

85. Stewart Armstrong, How We're Predicting AI, from the 2012 Singularity Conference.

86. Ji Shisan, The End of Work?, The New York Times, Opinion/Turning Points, December 10, 2015.

87. Joseph A. Schumpeter, Capitalism, Socialism and Democracy, London: Routledge, pp. 82–83.

88. Jaron Lanier, Who Owns the Future?, New York: Simon & Schuster, 2013.

89. Rory Cellan-Jones, BBC News/Technology, December 2, 2014.

90. Abraham H. Maslow, Farther Reaches of Human Nature, New York: Penguin/Arkana, p.269.

91. Psychology Today, Spirituality Basics, PsychologyToday.com.

92. Wikipedia, Unenumerated Rights, retrieved December 14, 2017.
93. Angie Peifer, The Purpose of Public Education and the Role of the School Board, National School Boards Association, August 19, 2014.
94. Kim Jones, What Is the Purpose of Education?, Forbes, August 15, 2012.
95. CollegeData.com, What's the Price Tag for a College Education, retrieved January 27, 2018.
96. Statista.com, Unemployment rate of recent graduates in the U.S. from June 2016 to June 2017, retrieved December 19, 2017.
97. Christopher S. Rugaber, Pay gap between college grads and everyone else at a record, USA Today, January 12, 2017.
98. Teresa Kroeger and Elise Gould, The Class of 2017, Economic Policy Institute, May 4, 2017.
99. Angie Peifer, August 19, 2014.
100. Ryan Craig, Bridging the Gap: New Models for Connecting Education and Employment, presentation to TAtech: The Association for Talent Acquisition Solutions, September 26, 2017.
101. Harold Myerson, The Forty-Year Slump, Prospect.org. November 12, 2013.
102. Baccalaureate, Online Etymology Dictionary (etymonline.com). retrieved December 15, 2017.

103. USHistory.org, Thomas Paine, retrieved December 21, 2017.

104. Wikipedia, Renaissance, retrieved October 30, 2017.

105. S. Hause & W. Maltby, A History of European Society. Essentials of Western Civilization, Vol. 2, pp. 245–246, Thomson Learning, Inc.

106. Dictionary.com, Theocracy, retrieved September 9, 2017.

107. Adherents.com, Largest Religious Groups in the United States of America, retrieved December 9, 2017.

108. Wikipedia, Ennoblement, retrieved March, 2018.

109. Ibid.

110. Laura A. Wallace, Peerage Basics, chinet. com, June 12, 2004.

111. Law Stack Exchange, What exactly is a "title of nobility" under the US Constitution? stackexchange.com, retrieved May 1, 2018.

112. Merriam Webster Dictionary, Talent, Merriam-webster.com, retrieved May 3, 2018.

113. Dictionary.com, Talent, retrieved May 3, 2018.

114. Sara Burrows, 85% of People Hate Their Jobs, Gallup Poll Says, ReturntoNow.net, September 22, 2017.

115. Shelly Prevost, 5 Reasons Why Most People Never Discover Their Purpose, Inc., August

29, 2013.

116. Michael Lipka and Claire Gecewicz, More Americans now say they're spiritual but not religious, Pew Research Center, September 6, 2017.

117. McCarroll et. al, 2005 p. 44 as noted in Wikipedia, Spirituality, retrieved October 30, 2017.

118. Steven Pinker, The Better Angels of Our Nature: Why Violence Has Declined, Penguin Group, 2015, p. 170.

119. Alexis de Tocqueville, Democracy in America, Bantam Classics, 2000.

120. Wikipedia, Me Too Movement, retrieved February 8, 2018.

121. U.S. Department of Labor, DOL.gov, Plant Closings & Layoffs.

122. Wikipedia, Enumerated Powers, retrieved January 17, 2018.

123. Jerry D. Marx, Great Depression: American Social Policy, undated, SocialWelfare.library. vcu.edu, retrieved January 23, 2018.

124. Justin McCarthy, U.S. Standard of Living Index Climbs to Highest in 7 Years, Gallup, January 8, 2015.

125. Marx, Great Depression.

126. Ibid.

127. Ibid.

128. Ibid.

129. Dan Brown, Origin, Doubleday, October 2017, p. 409.

Additional Sources

Liz Alderman, "Humans Wanted, Robots Accepted," The New York Times, April 17, 2018, pp B1, B8.

Robby Berman, "Your next job interview could involve playing a game against AI," big think, June 8, 2018.

Richa Bhatia, "Would Google's Guidelines For Ethical Use Of New Technology Halt The Development In Weaponized AI Industry?," Analytics India Magazine, June 8, 2018.

Steven Brill, "My Generation Was Supposed to Level America's Playing Field; Instead, We Rigged It for Ourselves," Time, May 28, 2018, pp 32-39.

Saheli Roy Choudhury, "Building an A.I. program is easy. The hard part comes after," CNBC.com, June 8, 2018.

Michael Chui, Nicholas Henke, Mehdi Miremadi, "Most of AI's Business Uses Will Be in Two Areas," HBR Technology, July 20, 2018.

Elizabeth Dias, "The God Squad," Time, June 19, 2017, pp 38-42.

Eightfold.ai Launches First Deep Learning Talent Intelligence Platform to Close the Talent Intelligence Gap, PRNewswire, Mountainview,

California, April 17, 2018.

Rana Faroohar, "Saving Capitalism," Time, May 23, 2016, pp 26-31.

Martin Ford, Rise of the Robots: Technology and the Threat of a Jobless Future, Basic Books, 2015.

Kevin Hartnett, "How a Pioneer of Machine Learning Became One of Its Sharpest Critics," The Atlantic, May 19, 2018.

Chris Havrilla, "Keeping Your Eyes on the Prize: A Parable for Leading AI / System Innovations," HRExaminer, June 6, 2018.

Kristen Houser, "Deep Mind Created a Test to Measure an AI's Ability to Reason," Futurism, July 13, 2018.

Neil Irwin, "Rethinking Low Productivity," The New York Times, Business, July 26, 2017, pp B1, B3.

Will Knight, "AI could get 100 times more energy-efficient with IBM's new artificial synapses," MIT Technology Review, June 12, 2018.

Sharlyn Lauby, "Everything #HR Needs to Know About Artificial Intelligence," HR bartender, June 10, 2018.

Farhad Manjoo, "In 2018, Expect Chaos to be the New Normal," The New York Times, The State of the Art, January 4, 2018, pp B1, B4.

Farhad Manjoo, "Government idle as Google builds future," The New York Times International Edition, Business, May 20-21, 2017, p11.

N. Gregory Mankiw, "Joblessness Way Down?

For Men, Add an Asterisk," The New York Times, June 17, 2018, Business, p3.

Jerry D. Marx, Ph.D., "Great Depression: American Social Policy," Eras in Social Welfare History/Great Depression, socialwelfare.library.vcu.edu.

Cade Metz, "Mark Zuckerberg, Elon Musk and the Feud Over Killer Robots," The New York Times, Sunday Business, June 10, 2018.

Shelly Palmer, "The 5 Jobs Robots Will Take Last," blog, March 5, 2017.

Shelly Palmer, "Stop Saying AI Can't Replace Humans," blog, May 13, 2017.

Shelly Palmer, "Machine Learning & AI: When to Start?," blog, May 21, 2017.

Jeremy Rifkin, The End of Work: The Decline of the Global Labor Force and the Dawn of the Post-Market Era, Putnam Publishing Group, 1995.

David A. Teich, "Management AI: Types of Machine Learning Systems," Forbes, June 6, 2018.

Roger Trapp, "How AI Can Help Leaders Make Better Decisions," Forbes, June 14, 2018.

James Vincent, "It's easier than you think to craft AI tools without typing a line of code," The Verge, June 12, 2018.

James Vincent, "Google unveils tiny new chips for on-device machine learning," The Verge, July 26, 2018.

Mindy Weisberger, "Can Machines Be Creative? Meet 9 AI 'Artists'." Live Science, June 1, 2018.

"What's Next," AARP.org Bulletin, June, 2018, pp 10-11.

Irving Wladawsky-Berger, "What Machine Learning Can and Cannot Do," CIO Journal, July 23, 2018.

About the Author

Peter Weddle is the Founder and CEO of TAtech: The Association for Talent Acquisition Solutions, the trade organization for the global talent acquisition technology industry. He is the author or editor of over two dozen books and has been a columnist for *National Business Employment Weekly* and the interactive edition of *The Wall Street Journal*. He is a graduate of the United States Military Academy at West Point and holds advanced degrees from the Bread Loaf School of English at Middlebury College and the John F. Kennedy School of Government at Harvard University.